THE PICTURE IN DESIGN

WHAT GRAPHIC DESIGNERS, ART DIRECTORS AND ILLUSTRATORS SHOULD KNOW ABOUT COMMUNICATING WITH PICTURES

STUART MEDLEY

THE PICTURE IN DESIGN

WHAT GRAPHIC DESIGNERS, ART DIRECTORS AND ILLUSTRATORS SHOULD KNOW ABOUT COMMUNICATING WITH PICTURES

STUART MEDLEY

Common Ground

First published in Champaign, Illinois in 2012
by Common Ground Publishing LLC
as part of The Image series

Copyright © Stuart Medley 2012

All rights reserved. Apart from fair dealing for the purposes of study, research, criticism or review as permitted under the applicable copyright legislation, no part of this book may be reproduced by any process without written permission from the publisher.

Library of Congress Cataloging-in-Publication Data

Medley, Stuart.
The picture in design : what graphic designers, art directors and illustrators should know about communicating with pictures / Stuart Medley.
    pages cm
Includes bibliographical references.
ISBN 978-1-61229-146-8 (pbk : alk. paper) -- ISBN 978-1-61229-051-5 (pdf)
1. Commercial art--Philosophy. 2. Imagery (Psychology) 3. Picture perception. I. Title.

NC997.M38 2012
741.601--dc23

2012004195

For Sam, Ben and Greer

Table of Contents

Foreword xiii

Overview xv

The structure of this book xvi

Introduction 1
    The absence of picture discourse 1
    A picture theory for graphic design 4
    Photographic realism 10
    Illustration and reduction in realism 12
    Perceptual psychology in design theory 14
    Interpretive understandings in design theory 17

Chapter 1: The Realism Continuum 23
    An abbreviated history of the realism continuum 24
    Representation and application 27
    Psychology of the less-real-than-real 29
    Conclusion 30

Chapter 2: The Psychology of Seeing 33
    The distant image 34
    The silhouette 36
    Simplest is best 37
    Schema 40
    Visual closure 41
    Gestalt 42
    The eyes and the brain have different tasks 44
    What the eye sees 45
    What the brain understands 46
    Caricature and the visual system 46
    A visual ideal 51
    The importance of synaesthesia in visual communication . 51
    In summary 52

Chapter 3: A History of the Picture in Graphic Design 55
    The Neutral Swiss: Modernism falters through prescription of
        photography 58
    Deconstructionist graphics 61

Zeitgeist: why deconstruction in 1980s? 65
　　　Pictures in contemporary design 66
　　　The new illustration 68
　　　Information architecture 73
　　　Conclusion 76

Chapter 4: Information Design **79**
　　Systems of Seeing
　　　Why simplified pictures work in complex communication 84
　　　Dichotomy between realism and diagram 85
　　　　Decontextual/contextual 85
　　　　Specific/general 89
　　　　Secretive/revelatory 90

Chapter 5: Visual Literacy and Pictorial Strategies **95**
　　　Visual literacy and the new illustration 96
　　　Picture-making without a brief 98
　　　Augmenting visual literacy 107
　　　Exemplars chosen along the continuum 109
　　　　The realistic picture 109
　　　　De-identified subjects 110
　　　　Depictions of the unreal 112
　　　　Caricature 114
　　　Silhouettes 116
　　　　Realistic outlines without interior detail 116
　　　Perceptual constancies 119
　　　　Line drawings with interior detail 119
　　　Gestalt closure 121
　　　Where picture meets type 123
　　　Type is picture 125

Conclusions **129**

Index **143**

Acknowledgments

Many of the thoughts developed in this book come from conversations I have been fortunate enough to have had with pictorial designers and illustrators from around the world over the last several years. I must acknowledge the time given to me by the following picture makers, and the profound thoughts they have shared which have shaped the direction of this text. My heartfelt thanks go to George Hardie, Roger Dean, Peter Grundy, Deanne Cheuk, Rilla and Steve Alexander, Patrick Thomas, Pedram Harby, and Elizabeth Resnick.

My sincere thanks go to my colleagues at Edith Cowan University: Christopher Crouch, for his encouragement and his rapid responses to my questions; Clive Barstow for the opportunity to write this book; and Hanadi Haddad for her support and assistance with the finer details in Chapter 2. To all staff at Otago University, I send my deepest gratitude for their friendship, advice and good humour. In particular I wish to thank Nick Laird, Scott Savage, Alex Gilks, Noel Waite, Kylie Patterson, Grant Baxter, Louise Mainville, Caroline McCaw, Gavin O'Brien and my dear friend Michael Findlay. Sarah Wakes and Mark McGuire deserve special attention for 'showing me the ropes' during my early attempts at research, as does Motohide Miyahara, for his enthusiasm, encouragement, his thorough commentary and his attention to detail, especially with regard to the psychological focus of this book. I must thank Paul Green-Armytage at Curtin University for his expertise on colour and for furnishing some key references. My heartfelt thanks go to Maggie Philips, at Edith Cowan University and Derek Kreckler, at Woollongong University for their early encouragement and advice, and for predicting the broad scope of this study. For showing me what design is really about I have to thank Professor Thomas Bley. My gratitude goes to the Professor also for the many important design network connections I have made since embarking on this project. Foremost among these is Professor David Skopec at Berlin's University of the Arts. His, as yet, unpublished *Iconicity* project rigorously examines the history of picture continua to a depth beyond the scope of this book. My sincere thanks also to Professor Arne Scheuermann for a fruitful discussion on how the content of this book might intersect with the excellent work on visual rhetoric by the Swiss Design Network.

I wish to thank Professor Yasmin Ta'an, of the Lebanese American University in Beirut for the opportunity to speak at Typographic Beirut 2005 about the research which has culminated here. My thanks also to Professor Teal Triggs, at London College of Communication and Associate Professor Laurene Vaughan, at RMIT University, for the opportunity to speak at Newviews2 in London 2008, and to run my ideas past Richard Buchanan, Rick Poynor and Gunnar Swanson in the same room at the same time!

Finally, I wish to say thanks to some particular students, past and present for all the things that they have taught me about design and illustration. Thanks especially go to Caleb Allott, Elika Satar Arjmandi, Nastaran Ghadiri Asli, Daryl Cowan, Jadwiga Daley-Thompson, Jane Dempsey, Daisuke Fukushige, Uriah Gray, James Hensby, Jarrad Grigg, Vaughn Hockey, Anita Koh, Silke Lösche, Abir Madani, Odireleng Marope, Rebecca Matson, Blagoj Micevski, Michelle Michael, Cam O'Connel, Matt Redway, Brendan Rich, Andy Simionato, Jessica Smith and Jody Williams.

Foreword

In your hands you now hold a book that may make the differences between Illustration and Design even less clear. There is no doubt that not only are most of the walls between these disciplines now tumbling, but that the frontiers between them should no longer be policed – particularly by writers, critics and publishers. In this book, among other considerations, Stuart Medley, and Common Ground undertake to provide a guide to this new territory without boundaries: an area of increasing interest to communicators and designers.

The book covers a history of the image in graphic design, the psychology of seeing, and investigates information design. It approaches these subjects from many angles. Medley's method involves listening to a proper variety of views: from stand points as different as Barthes, Gombrich and Scott McCloud; from psychologists, theoreticians, historians, critics, designers, artists and makers.

Medley carefully makes clear the gaps that need exploring within visual literacy and image evaluation. He argues well for the gradual narrowing of his remit, tightening up and editing his research with insight and originality considerably beyond mere listing or juxtaposition. The argument unfolds fluently. As a reader with both a professional and academic interest in Medley's subject and closely concerned with the making and assessing of visual communication I found this book a thoroughly engaging debate.

Many of his ideas were new to this reader but all Medley's positions and experiments are based on arguments between accepted views, and analysis of their shortcomings, synthesised into approaches of both practical and theoretical value. His critical insight is what enables this process and this is also in evidence when he finally starts to classify and explain examples in detail.

In the whole book he does this from three points of view: to provide and explain exemplars that underline the debate; to explain his findings and intentions to students and professionals about to commence a practical project; to help in unravelling and assessing students' and professionals' results.

Medley has rediscovered 'the realism continuum'. His use of it as a yardstick in considering examples is intelligent, and will be valuable to students and professionals.

Finally, with the carefully selected exemplars from international illustrators, and particularly his insightful analysis of their work, he completes the circle of finding, questioning, listening and observing began with a history of the image in graphic design, the psychology of seeing, and investigation of information design.

Where my personal interests touch Stuart Medley's is in the area of classification, recognition and distinction. An area that immediately follows the hunter-gathering (researching/collecting) that is essential to all graphic endeavours. A short collection of anecdotes, mostly based on books, and things that fly, and were brought to the front of my mind by this book, illustrates how this area affected my graphic life.

I grew up instructed and informed by two types of puffin, my brain was further mystified, and entertained by the two main colours of penguin (green and orange) and informed by pelicans (never forgetting my visual education which was undertaken by king penguins.)

Being informed at St Martins that there were a few salaried jobs for illustrators; in Museums and on expeditions: this because a realistic drawing could tell you more than a photograph. I have been told that the images that register the names of insects in the Natural History Museum are still drawings.

Formative was seeing a set of drawings of South American toucans which only undertook to distinguish between the species, not to mimic them. These were geometrically drawn and showed the different distributions of colour on a standard toucan. Compare and contrast with Edward Lear's wonderfully realistic engravings for John Gould's plates for *Birds of South America* (1830). Compare these with a set of sixteen nonsense birds possibly commissioned from Lear to teach a child his colours. Images of clearly distinct types of birds entitled; the black and white bird, the purple bird, the light green bird , all loosely drawn and water-coloured (1880). Compare again with 'an old man of Dumblane, who greatly resembled a crane.' A caricature for a limerick (1872)

I am immediately recognisable as not Naval at local parties near Portsmouth because of my plumage; I have a moustache and no beard. Edward Lear would pass muster.

A boy's book of watercolours of *Fighter Planes of World War Two* each carefully coupled with silhouettes that could be recognised; "Out of the sun at 3.00 o'clock!"

So now we come to the question about where, and on which shelf in your library this new book should now take up residence? This is a book by a practicing graphic designer, an image maker and a teacher and effectively plugs many of the holes between theory and practise. It would grace the shelves of professionals, students, critics, journalists, historians, theorists and teachers of graphic design, visual communication, illustration, typography, and information design. It is also an excellent picture book of course, and might need re-location for that reason alone. A good library might have to have copies under each heading and I suspect space should be left for further books covering the subject that Stuart Medley has introduced and clarified for us.

My copy might end up amongst the works of Edward Tufte.
This book will certainly help bring image further into the fold of graphic design theory.

George Hardie
Brighton, June 2012

Overview

The research upon which this book is based seeks to contextualise the picture within the field of graphic design for those interested in deliberate visual communication. As the role of pictures has not been a primary concern of graphic design previously, this book seeks to address the issue of how we see at a fundamental level in order to determine if that knowledge can help us to find means by which pictures may be evaluated. The seemingly unconscious nature of the act of seeing has meant that vision and pictures have been taken for granted in the field of graphic design. Questioning how we see will lead, in turn, to a more thorough understanding of the real tools of visual communication, the eyes and the brain.

This book is concerned with the following questions: Might the different levels of realism within pictures lead to different meanings? And, can the examination of image in terms of its relationship to realism also be a way of evaluating pictures for those interested in graphic communication? These principle questions lead logically to another: How is it that we can see and understand the less-real-than-real picture if we have evolved gazing at the real world in all its realistic detail?

This book does not argue that pictures are somehow more important than text. Rather, it acknowledges that graphic designers are visual people charged most often with communicating with and on behalf of clients, and that the designer might be presumed to be the more visually literate agent in this relationship. In this regard the book seeks to give to the designer some words to describe what goes on in pictures that are used for an intended message. Designers have had plenty of text to support their arguments for the use of a particular typeface or layout. Now they need words about pictures.

In this book I set out to explain why there can be a fundamental difference between realism and good communication. Beatrice Warde, in her celebrated essay, *The Crystal Goblet,* states that her approach to typography is a modernist purpose, to ask not how should typography look, but what is typography's function. To her its most important role is that "it conveys thought, ideas, images from one mind to other minds". She says, "it is important first and foremost, as a means of doing something" (2000, p.92). Here, I try to discover if the role of particular kinds of pictures can also be so described. This research may add to the growing interest in pictures and their communicative potential.

The structure of this book

This book is divided into an introduction and five chapters. In the introduction I will explore what has been discussed in graphic design theory and make clear that this discussion has continually side-stepped the role of the picture. In the few instances where the picture has been at the centre of graphic design discourse there exists confusion as to its role and effectiveness in communicating an intended message. Design, and illustration used within design contexts, are different to art in their intentionality. Graphic design and illustration are allied here: Visual forms created to express meanings to particular audiences. With regard to intentionality, graphic design has strong parallels with the visual literacy movement, which seeks "to understand and use visuals for intentionally communicating with others" (Ausburn & Ausburn, 1978. p.291). Accordingly, I examine some of the concerns of the visual literacy movement. I demarcate a wide gap in the theory so as to establish what a reduction in realism might allow in terms of visual communication. I study where models of understanding pictures have been built upon notions of realism and distance from realism, including the concept of the 'realism continuum'.

Chapter 2 is an attempt to establish whether realism is the best way to communicate visible aspects of the world to the human visual system; the eyes and brain. I will explain how this system can understand non-realistic pictures, and that it may even have a predisposition for such pictures. Further, I will examine some recent findings about the visual system concerned with the mechanisms of seeing, and through a study of the mechanics of caricature, how images are stored in the mind and then recalled.

In Chapter 3 I seek to discover how photography became the designer's *lingua franca* for pictures. I ask what has been the appeal of the photograph to the designer. In addition, I attempt to contextualise contemporary graphics in terms of their relationship to realism and in terms of the history of graphic design. This chapter will show that through graphic design's history there has been a general absence of any theoretical approach to picture use. The dominance of the photograph has only begun to weaken in favour of illustration in this last decade (Klanten & Hellige, 2005). This change is beginning to be reflected in the world's juried design annuals. This book asks if photographic or realistic pictures were ever the best way to communicate an intended message to an audience. I look at the use of pictures in visual communication, specifically in graphic design, to find out why this bias towards photography ever existed, and to see if this bias was warranted.

In my fourth chapter I deliberately target pictures on the opposite end of the realism continuum from photography to see what such pictures can help us understand about visual communication. Diagrams and information design programs built from pictograms are examined in terms of what these can show us about invisible (and therefore, unphotographable) relationships.

In my Chapter 5 I see if the research can be used as a basis to critique the role of certain pictures in graphic design. I need to demonstrate that a recent return to illustration does not mean the graphic design community and its audiences are newly aware of its strengths, but that these strengths need to be articulated so that illustration does not 'fall out of fashion', and designers again fall under the spell of photography for all graphic imagery. Exemplar pictures from along the realism continuum are examined in terms of what their distance from realism affords the visual communicator. This includes an examination, on the terms established by this book, of type as picture.

Introduction

This is a book which asks how we communicate with pictures. Specifically, it seeks to find out how best to choose or design pictures to convey an intended meaning. This is an aspect of graphic design that, for many reasons has been left alone by most design theorists, while typographic theory has been adequately explored and explained for graphic designers and educators. For reasons that will become clear, my approach in this book will be to explain pictures in terms of their distance from photographic realism. Realism and clear communication are two different purposes that only sometimes overlap. Paradoxically, it may be that one can communicate more accurately using less accurately rendered pictures. The easy answer to reach for is that realism creates noise in some communications. However, the real answer is far more interesting and compelling. I will get to grips with it in my Chapter 2. This book, in order to answer its own questions, is also something of a review of the knowledge gained in image theory within other fields, especially psychology, for its contextualised application here in graphic design theory. This is also a treatise on why illustration and diagram are so important in visual communication.

The absence of picture discourse

There is a good deal of books about type in graphic design theory but there is next to nothing about pictures.

INTRODUCTION

'Graphic design' may be thought of as a broad field concerned with the arrangement of type, pictures and other graphic elements in order to communicate particular messages. The predisposition of design theorists and educators, as well as design professionals, has been to concern themselves primarily with type and its composition, and secondly, if at all, with pictures. In the 1990s, graphic designers, theorists and educators began to loosen the grip of the Swiss School (Die Neue Schweizer Grafik) on graphic design practice. The prescriptions laid down by the Swiss modernists for typography were, at last, too constricting. Much was written at the time about what the 'young turks' of design were rejecting in the Swiss canon. Not a word was written or spoken about the Swiss prescriptions for pictures, the other half of the design equation. To this day, other than in the Swiss literature itself, nothing has been written about these pictorial prescriptions let alone rejected. Rather than the rich field of enquiry one might expect pictures to be within the discipline of graphic design, it is a field left largely barren of discourse.

Lupton and Miller in *Design Writing Research* (1999) are among the few to address this imbalance: "a divide persists between words and pictures, high academia and low mass media, authors and designers" (p.91). Even within design, a relatively picture-heavy discipline and a relatively new field for theoretical interest, the textual aspects are easily the most explored. Max Bruinsma, while editor of *Eye Magazine* remarked upon the 'second class' status of images when compared to text in visual communication:

> To acquire the status of serious conveyors of ideas, images still have to overcome the remainder of a 'class struggle' that is deeply embedded in our culture. There still is a marked 'upstairs, downstairs' division between images and words: words rule, images serve. [...] although to some it seems obvious that images are challenging the privileged status of words as the prime carriers of meaning, there is still considerable confusion about the ways in which this challenge can be met most effectively. (1998, p.3)

Perhaps *pictures* are not well understood by designers because the rules seem unclear. Certainly in this designer's experience, my colleagues like rules, as do I, as limitations to react against and to succeed in the face of, so to speak. Pictures seem to be far more elusive than type in regard to laying down laws to obey or to break. Part of the motivation for this book is to seek a set of guidelines that might apply to pictures used in graphic design. Beyond this search is a question about whether these rules can be explained effectively or with the certainty with which type is discussed.

Most writing about graphic design is in fact concerned with typography and layout only, and even these texts are few when compared with the amount of writing available on, for example, art history or literary criticism. Most likely this is a function of age. Design theories are few and far between because design, as a labelled vocation, is young. Design theory therefore, is even more of a newcomer to the rigours of academia. However, its struggle to enter this realm is itself the subject of at least some theory and discourse. Design theorist Gui Bonsiepe said, "In the field of design, intellectual formation has not a strong history, because design education grew out of craft training with a deep mistrust against anything theoretical" (2002, p.11). Donis A. Dondis, in her *A Primer of Visual Literacy,* speaks of "an unspoken devotion to nonintellectualism" in the visual arts (1973, p.11) and certainly in graphic design there is a paucity of research in general, and specifically research regarding pictures. Richard Saul Wurman, celebrated 'information architect' and instigator of the well-known TED Talks, sees an inherent shallowness in visual communication education and theory:

> As the only means we have of comprehending information are through words, numbers and pictures, the two professions that primarily determine how we receive it are writing and graphic design. Yet the orientation and training in both fields are more preoccupied with stylistic and aesthetic concerns [...] Despite the critical role that graphic designers play in the delivery of information, most of the curriculum in design schools is concerned with teaching students how to make things look good. This is later reinforced by the profession, which bestows awards primarily for appearance rather than for understandability or accuracy. (2001, p.30)

As I have said, graphic design textbooks concentrate on typography. For example, Meggs' *History of Graphic Design* (2006) describes the history of writing systems but not the history of picture making. Meggs speaks only fleetingly—about two and a half pages of his generous 200 page pre-amble—of picture-making as an urge of all prehistoric peoples. "In an engraved reindeer antler found in the cave of Lorthet in southern France, the scratched drawings of deer and salmon are remarkably accurate", he says, but follows immediately with, "Even more important, however, are two diamond-shaped forms with interior marks, which imply an early symbol making ability" (pp.6-7). This focus on lettering and, later, typesetting may be because words and lettering were historically held in higher regard, being the privilege of the wealthy and educated. As a result the precedents exist for writings about writing, albeit sometimes about the tools with which writing is made. Perhaps the prevalence of words is merely a function of designers, along with their fellow citizens, being a product of "twelve years of schooling in static print text" (Luke, 1994, p. 31). Or, as other critics of logocentric schooling—here Poracsky, Young and Patton in *The Emergence of Graphicacy*—have complained:

> graphics are viewed as 'too easy' or 'too simple.' Early elementary school books are full of pictures that complement learning and the newly acquired skill of reading. As the child progresses through school, however, fewer and fewer pictures tend to appear in books. (1999, p.107)

Fransecky and Debes, pioneers of visual literacy studies, in *Visual Literacy: A Way to Teach A Way to Learn* complain of this too: "Especially after the early grades, there is a tendency to minimize the visual aspects of communication and children are, in a sense, 'weaned away' from pictures and illustrations, from drawing and illustrating their own work" (1972, p.23). They tell us that: "For many years, schools have concentrated on the verbal skills—skills in reading, writing, speaking. The skills of visual literacy, though not recognized by this name, have traditionally been set aside as 'extras' or reserved for those with 'talent'" (1972, p.9). This problem exists too at tertiary level for the assessment of graphic designers, particularly at admissions interviews where typography is seen as a skill that may be taught (who can know the finer points of type before entering a design school?) but evidence of good picture making and composition are prerequisites. How many useful communicators does such an approach exclude? Mitchell (2008, p.15) talks more ominously about the 'pictorial turn' as a perceived threat to the status quo. As we shall see, this problem of words versus images will not go away, but in my Chapter 5, I analyse some examples of visual design that come to us from cultures where this 'weaning off' does not occur to see if these can show us something that we might otherwise have missed, especially in anglophone cultures.

While pictures precede words in prehistory, in the more recent past, and specifically in relation to their commercial application, type precedes pictures. Steven Heller, graphic design critic and author of many design books, including *The Education of an Illustrator,* reminds us, "In the beginning (of the early 19th century, that is), commercial advertising and graphic design relied on words because pictures were just too costly to reproduce." (2000, p.137). Perhaps suggesting that there is not much design theory about pictures because pictures are a more recent arrival in the graphic design milieu. Perhaps there are more of the typographically focused books merely because type is a more quantifiable, more easily measured science: It can be broken down into point sizes, line lengths and page proportions. For the researcher concerned with pictures in graphic design, apart from a very few, very recent publications concerned with illustration, the thread quickly leads outside of graphic design discourse and into art history, psychology and sociology.

A picture theory for graphic design

What should picture theory for designers encompass? Type theory is about choice of type appropriate to the communication task at hand. Picture theory for graphic designers might reasonably be expected to do a similar thing: provide a basis upon which pictures can be chosen for the communication task at hand. But how to choose? Bamford (2003) says there can't be a vocabulary of images since it would be as limitless as the imagination and graphic skills of humanity. But what if this search for a vocabulary is a red herring for graphic design? Type choice was never about *word* choice, so it is not about 'vocabulary': type choice is about the 'voice' with which the words are 'spoken'. From Beatrice Ward through Erik Spiekermann to Baines & Haslam, typography has been considered the silent voice through which words are 'spoken' in the head of the reader. Typography is less about *what is spoken* and more about *how it is spoken*. Similarly, picture choice for graphic designers need not concern itself unduly with image; with *what is shown*, but rather with pictures; *how it is shown*. It is not about vocabulary any more than type choice is.

Some definitions will make the previous statement clearer. In a standard dictionary, 'image' and 'picture' can be more or less synonyms. In the specialist discourse of design however, there is a licence and a need to make a clear distinction between the words. Image is *what's being depicted*, picture is *how it's depicted*: a picture fixes an image in a particular way. Mitchell describes this as the image-picture distinction: "you can hang a picture, but you can't hang an image". For example, an image of a bird in flight may be pictured through a photograph or it may be pictured through a water colour painting, a pencil sketch or a range of other means. These are different pictures of one image. This example perhaps focuses too much on media and less on conceptual depiction or even technique. As it turns out, as we shall see, the medium is less important to the picturing of the image than is the escape from the one medium that has dominated graphic design's pictorial space during its short history: photography. I will elaborate on this definition later. For now I want to say that this is a book about pictures rather than images. To develop the definition for designers, design educators, researchers and design students, for the purposes of this book: type is to words as pictures are to images. This way, there can be some equivalence between type and picture, as a means to frame the following research in a way that can be understood by disciples of a discipline which has long understood only one half of its own domain: type.

So, in trying to explore some equivalence between pictures and type that designers might understand, a logical place to begin is type and how it is classified. Typographic theory is all about rules, albeit rules to be tested and even broken once learned. In discussions regarding type a key issue is the designer's choice of type. Even the names of fonts purport to assist in the task of choosing. Galaxy Run, Entropy, Washout, Biffo, imply by their names, not merely their appearance, the uses to which they might be put; that there is a right and a wrong way of using them or, at the very least, that some uses are more appropriate than others. Indeed, to allow clear choice between faces, type is broken up into categories. Broad agreement can be found on some of these groups: Old style, Italics, Transitional, Modern, Egyptian, Sans Serif, Script. Some practitioners and theorists have railed against this way of organising type. For instance, Robert Bringhurst, author of *The Elements of Typographic Style* (1992) would have type distinguished by movements and eras, in the way that art and architecture are most often categorized.

Poised above all of these categories in type taxonomy are the two classifications, 'text face' and 'display face'. In the naming of these is the implication that the designer is about to make a choice that has significance. In other words, in spite of some disagreement regarding *how* type should be classified, it seems to suit type theorists to accept *that* type should be classified. Strangely, when it comes to pictures, the other half of the graphic design equation, such guidelines don't exist. The rules that designers seem to need to work within as regards typography are either not there for pictures or have not been defined.

Can there be a way of doing similar for pictures within the field of graphic design? Are pictures too difficult to classify or evaluate? What should designers know about pictures anyway? First, let's try to be clear about exactly what constitutes a picture. A useful starting point is to look at who has defined pictures before. The psychologist, J.J. Gibson, one of the foremost thinkers in the limited discourse in this area, says: "A picture is a surface that always specifies something other than what it is". For example, a piece of board is covered in paint, in patterns, shapes and colours until it begins to look like the bird in flight to which we referred previously. Perhaps a sheet of paper has some black ink precisely printed onto it until we see a series of visual instructions for the construction of furniture. Another, contemporary example might be liquid crystal cells which have been electronically activated to display the impression of a diagram upon the surface of a laptop screen.

Gibson goes on to explain that: "A picture is also a record. It enables the invariants that have been extracted by an observer [...] to be stored, saved, put away and retrieved, or exchanged." While the picture as a record seems clear enough, the word invariant in this context stands for a complex concept related to the psychological term 'constancy' that will be explored later in this book. It is not an easy concept to explain to anyone because most of us take seeing for granted. In terms of making pictures, we can say that invariants are those aspects of what we're looking at that our brains know don't change even while our eyes are telling us 'they're changing'! The difference between the observed and the understood is captured by artists when they depict these invariants. It is these aspects of pictures that allow simple 'schema', discussed in Chapter 2, to work as communicative graphics. Gibson tells us that there are only two kinds of pictures. He begins by describing how these are made:

> The enormously complex technologies of picture-making fall into two different types, the photographic methods, which are only a hundred and fifty years old, and what I call the chirographic methods [10], which have been practiced for at least twenty thousand years. The former involve a camera with accessory equipment for the hand-eye system of a human observer while the latter involve a graphic tool of some sort for the hand-eye system. The invariants made available by these two ways of treating a surface have much in common but are not equivalent,

Furthermore, Gibson understood that the method chosen for depiction changed what was possible in the understanding of the image:

> What exactly is a picture a record of? I used to think that it was a record of perception, of what the picture-maker was seeing at the time he made the picture at the point of observation he then occupied. It can be a record of perception, to be sure, and a photographic picture is such a record, but the chirographic picture need not be. There are several kinds of non-perceptual experiences [...] and the artist can make a record of these just as well as he can of what he perceives. He can record imaginary things, from the probable and possible all the way to the most fantastic of his dreams and hallucinations. He

can paint his recollection of something that no longer exists. He can paint fictions. And even when he is perceiving, he is seeing into the past and the future to some extent, so that he captures more than the surfaces projected at the instantaneous present.

In other words, the choice of method enables different possibilities in communication. The camera tends towards the documentary, while the illustrative methods, Gibson's chirographic picturing, allow the artist to document the world, in a way similar to the camera, or to be completely free of the actual and to invent the content of the picture. That is, the artist can choose whether to record something that was seen with the eyes or to invent and record something that was 'seen' in the mind, or by implication, the artist may choose a point between these, or to make a picture that combines elements of both approaches. We might describe these approaches as producing high-fidelity pictures and low-fidelity pictures, and pictures in between.

In this book we'll call Gibson's categories *photographs* and *illustrations*: these are terms that art directors, designers, design educators and students will best understand and they fit exactly Gibson's categories of *photographic* and *chirographic*. It's interesting that these divisions exist in the nomenclature of design. They suggest that the difference is important to practitioners, and that the difference is understood on some level. However, as we shall see, the discourse surrounding pictures is otherwise couched in terms that are imprecise and unhelpful, not only to the uninitiated, but also to the seasoned practitioner who wishes to put to his or her client a more persuasive argument regarding picture choice for a particular task.

The Oxford English Dictionary defines a photograph as a picture made using a camera, in which an image is focused on to light-sensitive material and then made visible and permanent by chemical treatment, or stored digitally. An illustration is defined as a picture illustrating a book, newspaper, etc. or as a visual example used to explain a concept, event or thing. In this definition a photograph can be an illustration. For the purposes of this book, because the distinction exists in the field of graphic design, we will exclude photography from the definition of illustration and maintain the parallel with Gibson's *chirographic* category of pictures.

As Gibson observed, the possibilities with the latter kind of picture, the illustration, are virtually limitless, and certainly extend beyond merely recording something tangible in the real world. It is this picturing of the invisible, that has been especially overlooked by design theorists. In the fourth chapter I look at picturing that which is not visible in the real world and how this helps us communicate ideas about systems and relationships between things rather than just things themselves.

If we look at 'image' in the terms of the definitions above, we can say that an image may arrive from two places only: from the real, visible world, and from our minds. The first kind of image may be photographed or drawn in order to be captured and shared as a picture. The second can not be photographed but may be drawn, painted, and so on, to be captured and shared.

For the artist, the image that comes from the mind may not be fully clear until the drawing commences, and may evolve and change as the artist works.

In the twentieth century, art historians and psychologists grappled with the role of the artist in recording documentary images through drawing and painting. Gombrich, well known in the arts for his psychological analyses of picture-making, penned the ambitious Art and Illusion to express astonishment at the history of pictures. Namely, "why it should have taken mankind so long to arrive at a plausible rendering of visual effects that create the illusion of life-likeness" (2002, p.246). He is surprised at his own findings that crude schema precede a mimetic reproduction of the world, a conjecture he reinforces with reference to primitive and child art (p.76). This finding is echoed by R.L. Gregory in *Eye and Brain* (1977, p.114) who says, "From the evidence of child art, it seems to be remarkably easy for human beings to draw typical views of common objects, but difficult to draw atypical views, with the perspective associated with a particular viewing position."

For Gombrich this understanding seems to lie in a distinction between 'seeing' things in the real world, and 'knowing' something about them, including knowledge of schema through which things can be depicted: "in all styles the artist has to rely on a vocabulary of forms and it is the knowledge of things that distinguishes the skilled from the unskilled artist" (2002, p.247). Importantly, for Gombrich, the use of non-realist schema is allied with the need to make pictures that merely 'function in the narrative' (p.248). In other words, the artist may present aspects of the image in such a way that these presentations may be understood, and yet, at the same time, are not presentations that accurately match their real world equivalents. Gregory has something to say about this too, however, for him the realistic picture precedes the schemata:

> The symbols used for electronics since the beginnings of the [20th] century parallel the development of the pictograms of ancient languages. At first the symbols were realistic drawings of the components. Within a few years the electronic 'pictograms' became simpler: the emphasis was placed on the functionally important features of the components, while the outward shapes were lost. The symbols pictured their functional significance. Each symbol is a kind of abstract cartoon. (1977, p.114)

As we shall see this idea of 'function', common to both authors' understanding of why non-realistic pictures 'work', becomes an important consideration for the use of less realistic pictures in graphic design. Function, of course, being a 'driver' of modern design that also steers it away from modern art.

Let's look at these modes of depiction, the photographic and the illustrative, in terms of what has been said about them by theorists from a range of fields. For each of the above pictorial theorists, realism, and the schema that effectively stand in its place in other pictures, are intriguing problems of seeing that need serious investigation. Accordingly, we'll look closely at some design theorists where they have, on the few occasions, applied themselves to the problem of pictorial fidelity.

When I discuss realism in this book, I refer to attempts by picture makers to capture the look of the real world. For this reason I focus on photography as the principle means of attaining such realism. The question of realism or likeness has been raised in the field of art history. Gombrich (2002) and Arnheim (1954) have each made statements to the effect that realism does not necessarily equate to good art. Artists too have discovered that realism may in fact limit the possibilities of visual expression. Picasso, for example is just one of many 20th Century artists whose early work was quite realistic but whose later work, work for which he became renown, sought new ways of creating emotional impact denied by realism. Art shows us, at the very least, that realism and less realistic forms lead to different meanings. Graphic design is concerned with visual meaning and, more so than art, with didactic or persuasive meaning. Just as art has made a problem of realism then, even more so should graphic design.

Gombrich (1982, p.124) on the transposition of life into picture, says it must be "caught rather than constructed [...] Here, as in other realms of art, equivalence must be tested and criticised, it cannot be easily analysed step by step and therefore predicted". With due deference to his labours, I wonder if the remit of graphic design allows us to be a little more pragmatic in exploring such possible steps. Gombrich tells us that "The contrast between the prose and poetry of image making often led to conflicts between artists and patrons" (1982, p.158). Presumably because the patron was paying for something he thought he hadn't received. While art seems to have mostly freed itself of this relationship, graphic design (sometimes referred to as commercial art) is very much a part of such an economy. While the "poetry" of design is a good thing in that it may draw the reader in to engage with the work, perhaps prosaic explanations of how the poetry works might be in order if only to better communicate to the client that he or she has in fact got his or her money's worth!

Plenty has been said about photography. It has its own rich history and a relationship, not without friction, to art history, and its documentary aspects are well covered elsewhere. Not a great deal has been overtly expressed about photography in relation to graphic design even though, or perhaps precisely because, it is the *lingua franca* of pictures in this field. Little has been said about illustration either, perhaps because the virtually limitless ways of depicting outside of photography suggest that no words can encapsulate such a boundless field. You can't define the infinite. But what if previous attempts have been looking in the wrong direction? This book is about looking at what statements can be made about these pictures that can be consistently assumed.

In order to get to grips with these problems we need first to look at what's been done before and why it doesn't fully address for the graphic design community (and I include the client and the audience in that community) the problem of how pictures work. This is a problem for any discipline that needs to use pictures in an informed way. Gibson himself observed that while the science of language is well established, no science of depiction exists.

Photographic realism

At this point it is important to consolidate: where do the above theorists agree in terms of pictures and their relationship to realism? Specifically, what are the most realistic pictures, and which are less realistic and how do these understandings accord with Gibson's ideas about photography and illustration? Of course, what constitutes a 'realistic' picture, as Arnheim (1954) has observed, is open to conjecture:

> just as persons of our own civilization and century may perceive a particular manner of representation as lifelike even though it may not look lifelike at all to the adherents of another approach, so do the adherents of those other approaches find their preferred manner of representation not only acceptable, but entirely lifelike (p.136).

In our own 'civilization and century' however, their can be little doubt that the photograph is perceived as the most realistic medium. The photograph, as Susan Sontag tells us in *On Photography* (1977), "is not only an image as a painting is an image, an interpretation of the real; it is also a trace, something directly stencilled off the real" (p.154). It is this aspect of photography, its ability to actually capture in two dimensions the three dimensions of visible reality, that I am concerned with in this book. Of course, the advent of computer software enabling alteration to photographic pictures is often cited as a reason why the photograph is no longer 'stencilled off the real'. Nicholas Mirzoeff, in *An Introduction to Visual Culture* (1999) says:

> With the rise of computer imaging and the creation of digital means to manipulate the photograph, we can in turn say that photography is dead. Of course photography will continue to be used every day in vast quantities but its claim to mirror reality can no longer be upheld. The claim of photography to represent the real has gone. (p.65)

While this suggests that the veracity of the photograph is indeed questionable, it is pertinent here to discuss the general perception of photography as a device for capturing the visible world realistically, rather than whether this is a misperception. The eminent designer and illustrator, Milton Glaser has said:

> But never-the-less, there is this vestigial sense that because there was something real at one point that was photographed by someone and that it encapsulates a moment in time, that vestigial memory of what photography used to be, which it no longer is, still remains in people's minds as being, therefore, more realistic (2006)

David Hockney, perhaps as famous for his use of photography as for his painting, declared photography a compromised medium because of this potential for digital manipulation. He tells us, "You've no need to believe a photograph made after a certain date because it won't be made the way Cartier-Bresson made his. But you can't have a photographer like that again because we know photographs can be made in different ways." (Jones & Seenan, 2004). Green-Lewis in *Framing the Victorians, Photography and the*

Culture of Realism (1996, p.59) points out however, that from photography's inception in the mid 19th Century, the argument about its documentary veracity versus a staged and composite approach was central to its perceived progress as a communicative medium. In other words, the potential for distortion and fabrication has always been there and has always been the subject of debate. To return to Sontag:

> A decade after Fox Talbot's negative-positive process had begun replacing the Daguerreotype (the first practicable photographic process) in the mid-1840s, a German photographer invented the first technique for retouching the negative. His two versions of the same portrait—one retouched, the other not—astounded crowds at the Exposition Universelle held in Paris in 1855 (1977, p.86)

So how did photography ever get this aura of truth if it was questionable from day one? Simply because it can capture reality and do so without as much input from the picture-maker as other media. "However carefully the photographer intervenes in setting up and guiding the image-making process, the process itself remains an optical-chemical or electronic one, the workings of which are automatic", says Sontag (p.158). Indeed, in photography's infancy, those who supported it as a documentary medium argued that it should be used to capture the world as it existed precisely because it allowed that a shared vision of the world could, after all, be had (Green-Lewis, 1996, p.26). One could argue, through a study of the work of Eduard Muybridge for example, that photography can in fact show us what the eye can't see, rather than showing us the world as the eye sees it: Horses hooves do in fact leave the ground when the creature is galloping, a fact disputed before proven through photography. It is in this sense though, that the camera's ability to see beyond what the human sees only strengthens its mythic objectivity, as an apparatus unencumbered by the emotionally biased views of the human visual system. Indeed, from its early history accounts of photography tended to "separate the photographer from the photograph and empower the photograph as an independent print of the world" (p.7). And finally, for our purposes here, the manipulation of photography does not disprove its reliability to reproduce reality but rather emphasises it:

> The consequences of lying have to be more central to photography than they ever can be for painting, because the flat, usually rectangular images which are photographs make a claim to be true that paintings can never make. A fake photograph (one which has been retouched or tampered with, or whose caption is false) falsifies reality. (Sontag, 1977, p.86)

In terms of this book, the general, albeit vestigial, sense that photography can capture reality in a more independent way than other media makes it the most realistic means of picture-making. As we shall see shortly, in a comparison of measures of realism, it is also seen this way by a broad range of visual theorists, and in my own surveys of design students and practitioners, the photograph is consistently chosen as the most realistic among a range of picture types. What is always less clear is why this matters. For example, even Chip Kidd, perhaps the most celebrated contemporary book designer in the US, struggles to articulate this difference: "I became very enamoured of the concept of illustrating [covers of] fiction with photography as opposed to illustration, and I can't really tell you why other than I just thought it would make the stories seem more real." ("Art of the Book", 2006).

Illustration and reduction in realism

Illustrations are generally held to be less realistic than photographs. Generally speaking illustrations require at least some level of distillation or abstraction, some removal of realistic detail (McCloud, 1993, p.42). However, the clarity evident in the photographic discourse is absent for illustration, perhaps, as I said above, because the enormous range of pictorial approaches available through illustration is too daunting to classify. The many approaches to making illustrations allows them to be a mere step away from realism, or at a much greater remove. It is their inherent distance from realism that makes illustrations of interest in this book. While this would include all reasons for making pictures, including reasons obscured by the picture-maker, or perhaps obscure also to the picture-maker, I am concerned in this book with those makers who wish to send a message to an audience. It is possible, that the picture-maker who makes pictures in order to obscure meaning will not be well-served by this book, although I hope that most of the discussion herein would allow such a picture-maker to be more sure how to make meaning, and therefore to avoid doing so where s/he feels so inclined.

Art history can give us clues about the drawn or painted picture's potential: If we return to Gombrich, he will tell us, "The first prejudice teachers of art appreciation usually try to combat is the belief that artistic excellence is identical with photographic accuracy". He proceeds with a thorough explanation of the difference between illusionist and schematic art. References to a need to avoid realistic representation appear elsewhere in art theory: for instance, there seem to be artistic reasons to not use realistic perspective in some pictures, as outlined in this statement from de Sausmarez (2002):

> Its value as part of foundational training is questionable, since by offering the student a ready-made recipe for achieving an illusion of space it curbs his spirit of enquiry and he may find himself drawing by academic theory of spatial projection and control rather than from sensation or personal observation. Not only does its logic and operation imply one fixed viewpoint, thereby freezing the entire visual field into static rather than dynamic relationships, but its 'one-eyed' geometry rules out the sensation of physical involvement, body-felt interpreting of space and forms in space which has previously been described as an essential human concomitant of spatial experience and conception. (pp.60-61)

This alludes to cross-modal sensual experiences, or synaesthesia, which will be covered in Chapter 2. It is one of the many reasons given as to why realism is not appropriate for all pictorial communication. As with many works that touch on pictorial realism and abstraction, these helpful snippets of information are scattered and buried in works rather than being a principle and accessible focus of theory for those who wish to construct meaning with pictures.

One book which does focus on picture making is *The Education of an Illustrator,* Edited by Heller & Arisman (2000). This work claims to be the "first ever blueprint for teaching and practicing the dynamic art and craft of illustration" and to "fill a practical and an intellectual void for educators, students, and professionals in the field of illustration". The void certainly exists in terms of intelligent discussion regarding the strengths and purpose of illustration. The authors within ably identify that illustration as a stream of design education and as a practice is in something of a crisis. However, the crisis they speak of seems to be exacerbated by the fact that few of illustration's small and scattered voices of support can effectively articulate what illustration is for or how it might communicate differently from photography, to which, outside of this book, it is frequently compared. Claudia Mareis in her introduction to *Illusive,* an anthology of contemporary illustrators' works, says, "Illustration's self-perception lies precisely in its difference to photography" (Mareis, 2005, p.5). For all the strengths of the essays collected in *Education of an Illustrator*—including a cross section of practitioners' concerns about the state of illustration, insights into the inspirations and working practices of name illustrators, and some educational syllabi focused on teaching illustration—this central problem is not effectively solved. One of the essays within, Dugald Stermer's, *Teaching Illustration,* begins with:

> My misgivings were manifold, but probably first and second among them were my doubts that illustration can be taught, and that even if it can, could I teach it? [...] Those concerns are still very much with me, so reading on will not provide any resolution. (2000, p.97)

This is not an atypical essay in *Education of an Illustrator.* Very few of the contributors grapple with the issue of illustration as a series of choices, or consider that there might be, outside of an individual illustrator's style, a more pragmatic approach that might help a practitioner teach it or a design student learn why they might consider using illustration in their next assignment or in their impending career. There is little discussion of illustration in the wider context of design or in context with its competitor for editorial space, photography. Those authors that discuss it in this context mostly lament that they are the photographer's poorer cousins.

As Heller and Arisman (p. 30, 2004) point out in their later book The Business of Illustration, illustration and graphic design have grown from different roots: the former from fine arts and the latter from the printing trade. They argue that the kinds of people that take to illustration are different to those that lean by nature towards graphic design. I feel certain that they are right and that one might add that photographers approach what they do with a different mind set again. However, in no way do they argue that graphic designers should ignore what illustrators do. Accordingly, I seek to explain the picture (whether created by illustrator or photographer) in terms of how it matters in visual communication. Good graphic designers are quite clear about what constitutes good typography and have the verbal rhetoric to back up their choices in this arena. Noone would assume that every designer needs to know how to design letters and alphabets in order to use them, and I do not assume that designers need to know how to shoot or draw a picture. However, designers should know why to apply a particular typeface and they should know why to use a particular picture. Certain families of type look very similar to each other. It takes a trained and practised designer to easily spot the difference between Helvetica and Univers or Myriad and Frutiger, yet those same designers would state irrefutably that the design is affected by these subtle choices. Designers and art directors need to know about the subtle differences between kinds of pictures and to be able to articulate these differences to the less graphically literate. The prominent illustrators I spoke to while writing this book had clear opinions on the difference between what they do and what a photographer does. For example, for Rilla and Steve Alexander of art and design collective, Rinzen, drawing enables the creator to make exactly what is imagined, regardless of budget. At the same time, specifics can be avoided, allowing communicating to a wider audience. Following their clues, I seek to explain how the human visual system deals with the drawn picture as well as the realistic image. One of the problems that needs to be overcome in order that pictures can be used more carefully within the design milieu is a problem of perception. The role of illustration seems to be perceived as one that is less pragmatic and more intuitive or emotional than the requirements of graphic design will allow. Adrian Shaughnessy on DesignObserver has said, "during the 1990s, illustration's 'individual style' became a liability. Visual communication was colonized by tough-minded, business-driven graphic designers who gave their clients what they wanted: branding, strategy and the precision-tooled delivery of commercial messages" ("Graphic Design vs. Illustration", 2006). What this book seeks to do is to provide to graphic designers and art directors some rationale for using photography or illustration in their designs. In addition, I hope that it might provide, especially to illustrators, some words with which they can persuade designers and art directors to utilise their art when appropriate.

Perceptual psychology in design theory

Donis Dondis, in her oft-cited, classic design text, *A Primer of Visual Literacy* (1973), delves deeper into a picture's relation to reality, and perhaps more than any other graphic design theorist identifies that we might respond differently to differently rendered pictures of the same image. However, having identified the existence of this phenomenon which allows changes in meaning as reality is left behind, Dondis pays it only brief attention: "The more representational the visual information, the more specific its reference; the more abstract, the more general and all encompassing it is. Abstraction, visually, is simplification toward a more intense and distilled meaning" (p.74). Elsewhere, she touches on abstraction while discussing photography. She attempts to explain that all photographs have within them an underlying abstract composition:

> But the fact is this: even as we view a highly representational, detailed, visual report of the environment, there coexists another visual message, exposing the elemental visual forces, abstract in quality but packed with meaning, which has enormous power over response. The abstract understructure is the composition, the design. (p.80)

In this regard she agrees with art theorists like Kepes and Arnheim who talk of perception as an imposition of structure upon a scene or a picture. This is the classic gestalt approach to understanding pictures: that, as Kepes maintains, the delineation of discreet objects in the field of view, or the separation of figure from field, precedes any recognition of objects:

> Certain optical characteristics tend to be seen together as a spatial configuration. As we look at a greatly enlarged halftone screen [as in a picture composed of pronounced dots printed via the offset process, for example, in a newspaper], what we actually see are different sizes of black dots and different white intervals. But instantly we organise and group these visible differences. Some units of black dots are seen in one form; some in another. Some elements are seen together because they are close to each other; others are bound together because they are similar in size, direction, shape. Only after this instantaneous organization is achieved can one see the resemblance of the picture to a human eye [Figure 1]. This organization of optical belonging is more basic than the recognition of the objects themselves. (1944, p.45)

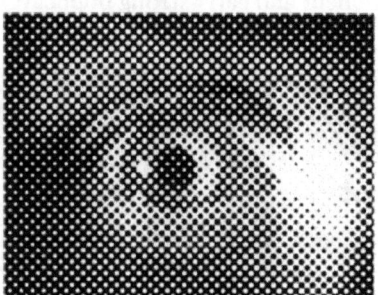 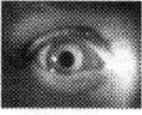

Figure 1: The enlarged picture clearly shows the arrangement of dots as the actual stimulus for our eyes; from these dots we perceive an eye. (Medley after Kepes)

Dondis goes beyond the gestalt approach and ventures into behaviourist territory in order to understand pictures. Like de Sausmarez above, with his concern for 'body-felt' understanding of space, she maintains that how we stand, move, keep our balance, protect ourselves; the way we react to light and dark or to sudden movement are factors in how we receive and interpret visual messages, though, unlike de Sausmarez she does not use this conviction to argue against perspective or realism: "The human organism seems to seek harmony, a state of ease, of resolution, what the Zen Buddhists speak of as 'meditation in supreme repose'" (1973, p.85). Dondis begins to shed light on the psychology of seeing further examined in my Chapter 3. She uses the psychologists' terms of "sharpening" and "levelling". Increasing tension or reducing it visually via composition or contrast, while still acknowledging the picture as a built thing; that elements of pictures can and should be rearranged, resized and repositioned until the satisfactory effect is achieved. The gestalt approach in general, and Dondis' in particular, attempts to define what can confidently said about all pictures and therefore looks at what all pictures have in common, namely, composition.

Implicit in this gestalt comprehension of underlying structure, but not explored by any of these authors, is that some pictures, even photographs, are more abstract than others. That is to say, the underlying structure will be more apparent in the picture the more abstract it is. The photographic examples Dondis gives (Figure 2) are themselves on the one hand quite abstract and graphic, and on the other at least non-specific enough (Where is this place? Who are these people?) to not refer directly to one thing or person. This makes the case for underlying structure easier to grasp. If the photograph is of a human face, especially one known to the reader, it is doubtful that underlying abstract structure would be as apparent or even relevant to the reading of the picture. In other words, the gestaltists are uninterested in the difference between the photograph's underlying abstract structure and that underlying structure being presented as an abstract visual. For Dondis, regardless of whether the visual message is a photograph or a graphic made of cut paper, "the process of composition is the most crucial step in visual problem solving. The results of the compositional decisions set the purpose and meaning of the visual statement and carry strong implications for what the viewer receives" (1973, p.20).

Figure 2: Dondis makes the case for the importance of underlying structure in any image

This ignores any difference in purpose or meaning that may be derived by choosing to present the image as say a line-drawing rather than a photograph of the same subject. An accurately shaded pencil drawing is visibly different to a photograph of the same subject; a line-only draft of the same subject is different again. In other words, as well as existing as designed compositions, pictures exist along a scale between representation and abstraction, and this results in a difference in meaning. The gestaltists tend to look for the image through the picture as if the picture did not mean so much by itself. Acknowledging this realism continuum may allow us to examine this difference.

Unfortunately, this narrow focus on underlying abstract structure as a universal *idee fixe* of everyone's perception has been seized upon by critics of psychological readings of pictures. They have reacted by rejecting out of hand any psychological understanding of pictures in favour of an interpretive or learned one.

Interpretive understandings in design theory

In Lupton and Miller's, *Design Writing Research* (1999) the view on visual language theories is that they rely too heavily upon perceptual psychology. Their criticism, which names Kepes, Anheim and Dondis, is that the assumptions of universal perception inherent in modernism, where these perceptual theories are firmly rooted, need to be addressed with a balance in design theory that leans more towards cultural and contextual understandings:

> Pervading these works is a focus on perception at the expense of interpretation. 'Perception' refers to the subjective experience of the individual as framed by the body and brain. Aesthetic theories based on perception favour sensation over intellect, seeing over reading, universality over cultural difference, physical immediacy over social meditation. Modern design pedagogy, an approach to form-making validated by theories of perception, suggests a universal faculty of vision common to all humans of all times, capable of overriding cultural and historical barriers. A study of design oriented around interpretation, on the other hand, would suggest that the reception of a particular image shifts from one time or place to the next, drawing meanings from conventions of format, style and symbolism, and from its association with other images and with words. While modern design theory focuses on perception, an historically and culturally self-conscious approach would center on interpretation. (Lupton & Miller, 1999, p.62)

As we saw earlier however, those design theorists that have focused on gestalt responses to composition, for instance Dondis, were themselves redressing a perceived imbalance towards text at the expense of image. Dondis is correct that the focus has been on type, and Lupton and Miller are correct that the focus of design theory has not been on cultural and temporal context. Neither criticism allows us closer to the problem at hand. Furthermore, in neuropsychology, perception is interpretation, but of *sensation*. Which is to say that perception itself is problematic and not to be taken for granted as the above interpretive view of design might suggest. I examine perception of images in Chapter 2. Helpfully, Lupton and Miller address the difference between the realism of photography and the abstraction of illustration elsewhere in *Design Writing Research*. They acknowledge the visual difference even though to them it is a function of politics: illustration looks like fine art and was pressed into service for high-brow goods until even this strata of publicity was mined by photography (1999, pp.72-89). Crucially, they address the question of specificity implicit in photography when they focus on stock pictures: "the informational richness and depth of the photographic image is at odds with the imperative for the generic" (p.133). They see the proliferation of these stock images as possible harbingers 'of a new kind of literacy'. Though they see these products beginning to 'look more and more alike'. This is as deep as they venture into the clash between specificity and generality which, as we shall see later, has been central to photography since its inception, but to which designers seem to have been blissfully unaware.

Roland Barthes, sheds a little more light in this area in his *Camera Lucida* (1982). He has this to say about the photograph:

> it is the absolute Particular, the sovereign Contingency, matte and somehow stupid, the This (this photograph, and not Photography), in short, what Lacan calls the Tuché, the Occasion, the Encounter, the Real, in its indefatigable expression [...] and suggests the gesture of the child pointing his finger at something and saying: that, there it is, lo! but says nothing else [...] A specific photograph, in effect, is never distinguished from its referent (from what it represents), or at least it is not immediately or generally distinguished from its referent (as is the case for every other image, encumbered—from the start, and because of its status—by the way in which the object is simulated). (pp.4-6)

For Barthes, the photograph always points to the very thing it was captured from and nothing else. As we shall see in Chapter 2, a less realistic picture suggests a less specific subject, as Dondis has suggested, and consequently allows for other meanings to exert themselves. Other leading lights in visual theory have dealt with the photograph, and some with its relationship to other kinds of pictures, but no-one seems to deal specifically with the differences in meaning allowed by the different depictions.

John Berger (especially in *Ways of Seeing*, 1974) is useful in pointing out that the perspectival way of depicting the world is not a natural way of apprehending but in fact a cultural construct. This notion is significant in this book especially since it provides a rare bridge between the psychological theory—joining seamlessly with R.L Gregory's elucidation of 'object constancy' as a psychophysical phenomenon which overrides the effects of perspective—and the cultural theory of the picture; between what Lupton and Miller describe as the perceptual versus the interpretive approach to understanding pictures.

Generally speaking, the interpretive approach, as set out by Lupton and Miller, seems to identify the issue at the centre of my research problem, that pictures using different levels of realism communicate differently, but not to be able, or to be uninterested in trying, to explain it. Charles Peirce for instance, founder of one of the two main branches of semiotics, has it that the 'index' has a clear visible connection to its referent that seems unproblematic. In Morris (1938), semiotics are broken into the categories of syntax, semantics and pragmatics; the syntactic being the level which presupposes any recognition of the picture (Goldsmith, 1984, p.124). These levels have echoes in Barthes' categories of denotation, connotation and myth.

For Barthes, the 'denotative' order comprises the visual stuff that we can easily describe. This first order of signification is taken as read; as if it requires no effort to perceive.

A semiotic perspective has been used to examine the role of the picture in promotional and advertising design. Berger (1972), Barthes (1978) and Kress and Van Leeuwen (1996) make politically charged problems of interpreting such pictures. Their approaches favour an interpretive and subjective view of pictures over perception. Of course, designs can be and are targeted at particular cultures, age groups, and sexes, but the assumption of completely unique individual readings is anathema to commercial design. For these reasons: that the interpretive theory is covered elsewhere, and that it implies a unique interpretation by each viewer, I will not take such a view. It is my experience as a commercial graphic artist and a teacher of graphic art that design needs at the very least to explore assumptions of universality since every designer is seeking to reach an audience of at least some number. Design is different to art in its intentionality. Gui Bonsiepe and Thomas Maldonado at the Ulm Hochschule für Gestaltung (Ulm HfG) attempted to explore the shared effects of visual communication by examining the picture within the realm of rhetoric. However, like other semioticians, they focused on the parallels between speech, writing and picture making. In their paper, *Design as rhetoric, basic principles for design research*, Joost and Scheuermann further develop the ideas from the Ulm HfG and, crucially from my point of view, they state that design operates as rhetoric in its own right, "it is not about transferring patterns, figures or processes, piece by piece, from the rhetoric of speech" (p.157). They argue that design, like all rhetorical expressions, "is based on strategic communication decisions, which aim for effectiveness" (ibid.). I hope that some of the findings in this book can be used to hone the rhetoric of design. This view of design also has strong parallels with the visual literacy movement. Later in this introduction I inspect where the visual literacy theorists have explored the importance of reductions in pictorial realism. It may be impossible to be apolitical while seeking to construct visual communication theory, however, I hope that the ideas expressed in this book will enable not just those designers and illustrators working in the commercial realm to 'shift more units' on behalf of their clients, but also enable designers working towards socially sustainable ends, in the not-for-profit sector and in graphics of protest to better target their visual communications.

I acknowledge that there are limitations with my approach to the topic of pictures in graphic design. This book will concentrate more on perceptual responses to pictures since these have been examined elsewhere with regard to general design composition and art but are underexplored with regard to their place in graphic design.

Maria Nikolajeva and Carole Scott, in *How picturebooks work* (2006) say of understanding pictures with text, "analysis starts with the whole, proceeds to look at details, goes back to the whole with a better understanding, and so on, in an eternal circle known as the hermeneutic circle. The process of 'reading' a picturebook may be represented by a hermeneutic circle as well" (p.2). In this way the reader of picturebooks can look at the text then the pictures, or vice versa, or s/he can dip in and out of each, apprehend the whole page or read using a combination of these approaches. Given that graphic designs, like picturebooks, are generally comprised of type and picture, my exploration of pictures in graphic design will be via an artificial separation of image from text. However, this too can be regarded as a part of the hermeneutic circle in the hope that, with a better understanding of pictures and their role in design, someone in the future can come back to addressing the whole. The understanding of text has been very thoroughly addressed through literary analysis on the one hand (for content) and typographic theory on the other (for form). It is the picture in visual communication that requires the intensive care and hence its temporary removal here from type.

Of course I am simplifying and generalising the semiotic position on picture interpretation. As with the Modernist art and design critics, there are a range of positions taken on denotation and connotation. In Hall (1980, p.132), the photographic 'signifier' is allied exactly with its 'signified', in the same way that Dondis, Sontag and Lupton talk about a photograph being specific to its subject. Barthes, on the other hand, came eventually to regard denotation as a pretence of pictures: "denotation is not the first meaning, but pretends to be so; under this illusion, it is ultimately no more than the last of the connotations (the one which seems both to establish and close the reading), the superior myth by which the text pretends to return to the nature of language, to language as nature" (1974, p.9). In a sense, the concern with pictures in terms of how realistic they are is implied: Presumably most semioticians and interpretive theorists would see the highly realistic picture as having more of a consensus among viewers than an abstracted picture.

Once upon a time the picture was central to an understanding of graphic design. If, as Heller (1999) contends, graphic design began with the art poster, then we can see that Lautrec, the Beggarstaffs, then later, Abram Games, and Lucien Bernhardt were at the leading edge of the practice. Later, in the 50s, the Swiss typographers even had specific prescription regarding the picture's role in graphic design and the kinds of pictures that were right and proper for communication tasks (more on that later). I want to put the picture back on the graphic design agenda. But we need a way to teach it and to communicate its importance to clients—we need a means to evaluate and explain it. This needs to be rather mechanical if it is to suit a profession used to dealing with the quantifiable measures such as point sizes, line lengths, leading, etc.

I do not intend that this book replaces the sophistry of semiotics, but rather for it to prefigure a semiotic analysis of pictures in design: to make a problem of the act of seeing before deciding what individual pictures mean. Historically the semioticians tend to be more interested in the 'higher' levels of signification since these seem rich with interpretive possibilities, but as we shall see in Chapter 2, the 'denotative' level is problematic and interesting in itself. Of course pictures are context sensitive as are words, but the theory that examines that aspect of vision has already jumped over a problematic area. While the semioticians' interest in these more connotative pictures should increase as the images are further removed from a general consensus, via a reduction in realism, still they remain unconcerned with how we are able to perceive these abstractions in the first place.

Perhaps in part because of the division between photographic and illustrative means of making pictures, discourse has tended to lump all illustration in together. On the one hand, this is helpful in that once realism's stranglehold has been broken by the picture-maker who avoids photography, a range of possibilities arise. However, on the other hand, one, catch-all phrase is less than helpful since this range of possibilities is so broad. If we consider all pictures on a sliding scale however, we can start to examine different affects in terms of a picture's relationship to realism. The degree to which a picture can capture, as Gibson said, "more than the surfaces projected at the instantaneous present" is proportional to its distance from realism. As it turns out, a whole raft of other interesting things begin to happen when picture makers move away from realism. The thing to do next is to look at this sliding scale to begin to evaluate pictures in a way useful to graphic design.

Chapter 1
The Realism Continuum

We have seen in the introduction to this book a separation in picture theory between photography and illustration, a distinction reinforced through separation of disciplines in art schools: photography from drawing and painting; technical drawing from illustration, and so on. I wish to re-unite these modes of depiction here in terms of their relationship to pictorial realism. An easy way for us to understand pictures is to classify them along a continuum. Broadly speaking, the realism continuum is a visual model that presents any image as a series of pictures, each iteratively reduced in fidelity from its referent. An example of a continuum can be seen at Figure 3. I will explain as we proceed that different theorists have, for a range of reasons, posited different variations of this general idea. All agree that the different points along their proposed continuum offer up different possibilities in visual communication. Firstly, I will cover the history of this model and its uses: for example, a continuum has been used before to gauge the effectiveness of educational instruction (Gropper 1963; Knowlton 1966; Dwyer 1972; Wileman 1993) and to explain the communicative potential of different drawing styles (McCloud 1993). Secondly, I will explain that several theorists have described the difference in communicative potential of the different distances from realism. In addition, scattered reference is made in design theory to less detailed pictures being easier to scan for pertinent information and generally reducing demand on working memory (Malamed, 2009).

Fig. 3: An Example of a realism continuum (Medley after Wileman, McCloud, et al)

An abbreviated history of the realism continuum

While Gibson and Gombrich had long been interested in the separation between the accurate illusion of life and the abstraction of the visible world, *A Guide for Improving Visualized Instruction* (1972, p.95) is the earliest work to directly suggest a 'realism continuum'. In it, Dwyer makes a table of the variables to be taken into account when considering illustration for instructional use. His term, 'illustration', means pictures used to support an instructional text or verbal commands. As such, the term includes photographs. His table includes *Educational objectives, Student characteristics, Method of presentation, Type of visual,* and *Cueing techniques*. Of these, it is the *Type of visual* variable that alludes to the levels of realism used in illustration, and that pictures may be chosen by this criterion. Indeed, in a later study, (1979) Dwyer refers to the 'realism continuum' as just such a measure of *type of visual*. The limitations of Dwyer for my investigations are that he was concerned only with realism. His continuum ends at realistic line drawings rather than heading further in the direction of distillation or abstraction. To look further along this continuum we need to explore the work of other visual communication theorists. Wileman, in *Visual Communicating* (1993) attempts to cover the whole gamut of picture types in terms of their level of realism. His linear scale runs from 'concrete' at the realistic end to 'abstract' at the distilled end. Wileman (p.12) places along this scale a handful of different picture types as examples. He states that "There are three major ways to represent objects—as pictorial symbols, graphic symbols, or verbal symbols". These categories are based in part on Rudolph Modley's categories for graphic symbols (Modley, 1976). Note, that Wileman covers in his first category, 'pictorial symbols', those pictures with which Dwyer was concerned in total. Wileman continues,

Pictorial symbols are produced as photographs, illustrations and drawings. All of these are attempts to represent the object or thing as a highly realistic and concrete symbol. The viewers should easily be able to translate a pictorial symbol to a real world example. (1993, p.11)

Using his model, Wileman found, somewhat surprisingly, that the most realistic pictorial symbols were rarely likely to be the most readily identified. In essence, his work echoed findings in Goldsmith's *Research Into Illustration*(1984) and Gombrich's *Art and Illusion* (2002) that the most realistic picture is not the most communicative. More on that finding later.

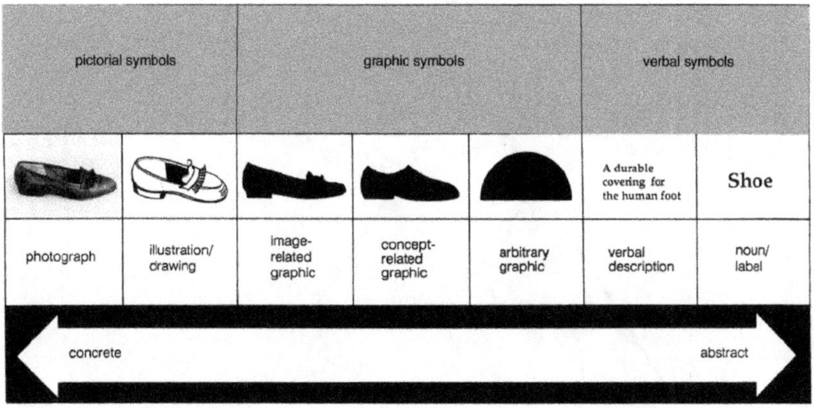

Fig. 4: Wileman's 'Concrete to Abstract' Continuum

McCloud (1993) goes further than any of the previous theorists in using the continuum concept. He is particularly focused on the visual presentation of comics characters and what a move away from realism entails in this regard: "When drawing the face and figure, nearly all comics artists apply at least some small measure of cartooning. Even the more realistic adventure artists are a far cry from photo-realists" (p.42). McCloud's model, in *Understanding Comics*, does not echo Wileman's approach, but contradicts it in more than one aspect. Attempts to reconcile the two approaches are difficult. In contrast to Wileman, McCloud has 'abstract' on a separate axis to 'concrete' (Figure 5). McCloud's scale of realism goes from 'concrete' to 'iconic' along the x axis. While it seems perfectly logical to pare away detail a little at a time to create a reductionist picture from any given image, to jump from this linear path to a purely symbolic picture seems to break with that logic. Things become more 'abstract' for McCloud perpendicular to this scale, along the y axis. He declares that "iconic abstraction is only one form of abstraction available [...] usually the word 'abstraction' refers to the non-iconic variety, where no attempt is made to cling to resemblance or meaning [...] this is the realm of the art object." (pp.50-51) However, McCloud puts writing on this same x axis as the realistic picture. It is not explicitly divulged why writing, a purely abstract form of visual communication, belongs on McCloud's iconic realism continuum while abstract pictures do not. Gregory (1970), Feldman (1976) and several type historians have explained alphabetic characters as derivations of representational pictures, so it seems appropriate to consider them on this iconic realism continuum. In that sense too, the abstract, non-alphabetic image, most likely, once upon a time, to have derived its shape from something witnessed in the real world belongs along here too. The fact that these, like letters are no longer directly connected to their visual roots ('A' derived apparently from the bull's head, for example) does not mean they are not abstractions of them.

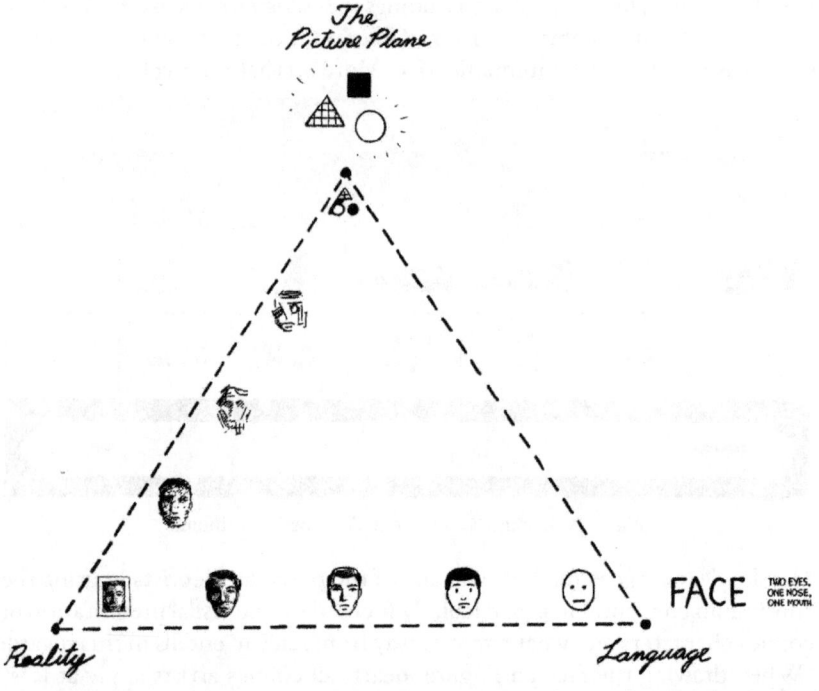

Figure 5: McCloud separates Non-iconic Abstraction from Iconic Abstraction and Text

In McCloud's own subtitles for his continuum, he seems to make an argument along these lines. Beginning with what he describes as a scale of 'iconic-abstraction' (p.46), he describes what is happening along this scale; what other researchers regard as an 'increase or decrease in detail' (Dwyer, 1979, pp.19-25). McCloud resolves that this lessening of realism results in not one, but several changes in communicative potential, by subtitling his scale as *Complex to Simple, Realistic to Iconic, Objective to Subjective, Specific to Universal*, closely reflecting Lilita Rodman's (1985) concept that abstraction moves images from the particular to the generic; from a focus on surface to a focus on structure; and from mimetic to symbolic, that is from being a high-fidelity copy of the physical appearance of the thing to a distilled, low-fidelity approximation.

It is worth remarking that McCloud and Wileman both postulate that the continuum should contain words, reflecting Mitchell's observation: "it isn't that words and images exist in separate compartments, or that they only interact as antagonists. One of the key things about language is that images come bubbling up inside of it" (2008, p.25).

Wileman's line progresses from *photograph* through *illustrated drawing*, to *image related graphic, concept related graphic, arbitrary graphic* (note, Wileman acknowledges and accommodates this arbitrariness), to *verbal description*, and *noun label* (1993, p.12). Wileman and McCloud's scales do not coincide at this textual end. For McCloud, the *noun label* precedes the *description*, his reason being that individual words, especially those presented with graphic 'punch', are closer to pictures than the more elaborate prose of a description (1993, p.48).

The concept of the continuum exists in a few other theorists' work, but is never as overtly articulated as in these above. Graphic design theorist Meggs' (1992), effectively follows Wileman in terms of his classification of possible picture types. Meggs refrains from labelling this as a continuum however, and he does not follow Wileman or McCloud so far as to go into text territory. Like Wileman, Meggs includes arbitrary abstractions, and like McCloud, and Dondis (1973), he recognises that less realistic pictures become less specific. Beyond this however, he makes no mention of how these approaches to picture making relate to each other. Rather, his list appears to be a basic taxonomy of picture types: "Images are pictures of all kinds ranging from simple pictographs to illustrations and photographs" (p.19). Gombrich had a notion of the realism continuum, but did not to set it down in a diagram: "however we interpret the facts, it remains true that all representations can be somehow arranged along a scale which extends from the schematic to the impressionist" (2002, p.247). He is interested in the pull to the more distilled end of the scale as the natural impulse of the artist. Smerdon is cited in Kiefer's *The Potential of Picturebooks* (1995) as using a conceptual continuum to ascertain children's preferences for realism and abstraction. Generally, Smerdon found that the older children preferred art that was more realistic. Kiefer disregards Smerdon's study however, for, among other things, 'meddling' with the art in its original form, for instance, by removing colour from the pictures shown to his sample groups.

Representation and application

Generally, the theorists who have used a continuum model suggest that the way things are represented, how realistically or otherwise they are depicted, affects how images are received, and therefore the meaning gained from them. The importance of matching a visual representation to a desired outcome is already acknowledged and taken advantage of in fields such as animation (Coco 1995; Robertson 1995), character-agent design (CA, embodied agents e.g. Ananova, Adele, Steve) (Haddad 2005; Wonisch & Cooper 2002) film and television (Philpot 2000), art (Preble & Preble 1994), simulation (Johnson, Rickel & Lester 1999), visualisation (Robertson 1997; Digital Humans, in Wired 1996), robotics (Wolfson 2001) and computer-based instruction (Dwyer cited in Allessi & Trollip, 1991) to name a few.

Various studies into levels of abstraction in representation indicate influence upon user/reader/viewer affective response as well as information delivery effectiveness (Haddad 2005; Koda & Maes 1996b; Schumann et al. 1996). A significant number of studies and literature recommend that less accurately rendered visual representations are more effective communicatively. This is due, but as we shall see only in part, to less distraction associated with the over-reading of unintended messages because of presentation complexity (Wilson 1997; Dwyer cited in Allessi & Trollip, 1991). As to the other reasons why realism is problematic, *the reasons why complexity itself is problematic*, we need to wait until the next chapter. In reference to Communication Theory (Figure 6) (Berlo 1960, drawing on Shannon and Weaver) it can be said that more realism creates more noise (distraction) from high user expectation and unnecessary cognitive activity about the picture itself.

S M C R

SOURCE   MESSAGE   CHANNEL   RECEIVER

Figure 6: Berlo's SMCR Model of Communication (Berlo1960)

Haddad's study (Figure 7) into three iteratively reduced pedagogical talking head character-agents (CAs) suggests that detail found in realistic pictures that is not pertinent to the context or the message being delivered may be regarded as noise in any communication. Where source, message and receiver are constant, a channel with noise (distraction) is less effective than one without noise (Bello 1953). More specifically, communication theory provides that the clarity or fidelity of information passing through a visual representation to the user can be influenced by distraction (interference or noise) generated by that picture. Connie Malamed, in *Visual Language for Designers* (2010) says the cognitive advantages of low-fidelity graphics include that these allow for quick visual scanning and less information processing, for example, while following instructions.

Although there is a growing awareness of the differences of representation and their uses, it is a little explored area in terms of classification, measurement or diagnostics, especially within the graphic design field.

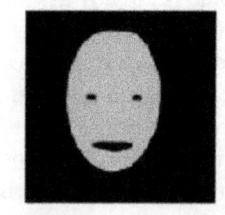

Figure 7: Iteratively Reduced CAs – Iconic Photorealistic, Iconic Schematic and Abstract Schematic Along the Image Continuum (Haddad 1995)

Psychology of the less-real-than-real

None of the above texts however, explains how it is we can see the less-real-than-real in the first instance. Two aspects have been missing from the history of this discussion. Firstly, how can we perceive pictures more reduced in referential content? Secondly, and following on from this first question, what tasks of perception do the different levels of realism and abstraction help us with?

The Two Ends of the Line, and the uses to which their pictures can be put

The continuum theorists above assume a linearity, not just in the iterative reduction of detail from the original photographic capture of an image but also in the way this reduction causes the pictures along the continuum to change in communicative function. For example, McCloud sees the continuum as serving to describe pictures as *Specific to Universal*, and so on. This implied linearity of function would suggest that pictures become progressively better at communicating some things and worse at others as they are chosen from one end to the other along the continuum. However, McCloud's measure of *Objective to Subjective* along the continuum, is arguably refutable. At least one designer, Josef Müller-Brockmann, would endorse photography, from one end of the scale, for its communicative objectivity, while another designer, Otl Aicher would champion the use of the highly distilled pictograms, the kind of pictures found at the other end of the continuum, also for their clarity and objectivity. These latter pictures are elemental components of information design. A field of design that theorist Robin Kinross (1989) describes as projecting the rhetoric of neutrality.

Indeed, there appears to be empirical evidence to suggest that this linearity of affect along the continuum is confounded in particular circumstances. Fussel and Haaland (1978) describe how they put visual tests (containing pictures of "common objects" such as a tree, people, a chicken, etc.) before some 400 Nepalese adults who were unused to pictures. The study was done in order to prepare materials for instructional booklets for nonliterate people. The study group was shown 10 different things presented in six different styles. These styles, from realistic to distilled, comprised *black and white photographs*, *black and white photographs with background removed from around the subject ('blockout')*; *a line drawing with shading and internal detail (a 'three-tone' picture)*; *the same drawing without shading and with minimal interior detail*; *a silhouette*: and *a line drawing*. Cumulative correct responses to all 10 of the pictured subjects were as follows: Three-tone, 72%; Blockout, 67%; Line drawing, 62%; Silhouette, 61%; Photograph, 59%; stylised drawing, 49%. The authors conclude that:

> the lessons to be learned from this part of the study would seem to be that the more detailed and realistic a picture is, the more effective it is. The so called 'simple' stylised drawings are evidently not simple in anything but appearance, making greater demands on the person trying to interpret them. (p.27)

However, the authors do not make special mention of the photographs, the most 'detailed and realistic pictures' in the sets as having performed the worst bar the stylised drawings. It is by no means a simple progression towards realism that will solve their communication problem since the most realistic of the picture sets performed almost as poorly as the least realistic, and the best performing sets of pictures in terms of realism actually lay in between these two extremes. Dwyer observed, following one of his studies, that an increase in the amount of realistic detail contained in an illustration will not produce a corresponding increase in the amount of information a student will assimilate from it (Dwyer, 1972, pp. 89-90). However, he also found that "The use of specific types of visual illustrations to facilitate specific types of educational objectives significantly improves student achievement of externally paced instruction" (Dwyer, 1978, pp. 96-97).

Conclusion

Clearly this discussion concentrates on perceptual responses to pictures rather than on the role of interpretation. My bias comes in part from a graphic design background where practitioners in the discipline are generally trying to reach a wide audience. The bias is adopted in order to establish whether we may confidently agree, as a design community, on the ways pictures communicate because of their relationship to realism; to ascertain what we have in common in terms of perception before we decamp into visually interpretive factions. Further complicating this issue is that perception, as psychology would have it, *is* interpretation: of sensation. From experiments conducted with students of varied international backgrounds (Medley, 2009), however, the realism continuum model does seem to have some universal currency. When students were asked to place, from most realistic to least, half a dozen different, unlabelled representations of the same object along a continuum, the responses were uniform. Again, however, we must acknowledge that design students are not laypersons when it comes to the image. Training in aspects of picture-making can change the way one perceives pictures (Noide, et al, 1993, p.219).

Each of these continua are helpful models to begin categorizing pictures, but it should be remembered that they are open to criticism for various reasons. For example, at Figure 4, it can be argued that the silhouette with detailed outline belongs in the pictorial symbols category since its appearance is a function of lighting conditions rather than any iconic or symbolic abstraction. That is, a silhouette can occur in the real world; the visual world unmediated by drawing. In other words, it can be an image before it is made into a picture. The silhouette is closer to the colour photograph in that it too can be captured from the real world using a camera. On the other hand, the detailed line drawing is closer to the colour photograph in that it may contain nearly as many salient details as the photograph.

The continuum is also a rather blunt instrument. Choices, in reality, don't lie neatly along a spectrum, arranging them so is merely a convenient organizing principle. In the fifth chapter I show that 'unreal' images can be placed at the real end of the continuum.

Perhaps the progression along the continuum is problematic because the visual system has more than one task to perform. Psychologists talk of 'Object constancy' and 'homogeneity' problems (Rhodes, 1996). What these mean, respectively, are 'what kind of object am I looking at?' and 'which one of those particular objects am I looking at?'. The first is a more coarse problem of differentiating between classes of objects; is that a car or a house? The second is a more fine-tuned question intended to differentiate between objects within the same class; what model of car am I looking at? Or finer still, which particular person am I looking at? I propose that the coarse problem is more effectively dealt with by communicating with less realistic pictures, and the fine problem more effectively dealt with using pictures higher in detail, more closely matching their real-world referent. The way that the human eyes and brain deal with these problems is the focus of the next chapter, and the crux of the issue with which this book is concerned.

Having looked at some of the ways that different levels of fidelity affect visual communication, we need to look more closely at how it is that we see in the first place those pictures which are reduced in fidelity from the very realistic.

Chapter 2
The Psychology of Seeing

In the previous chapter I acknowledged the general principles of Shannon and Weaver's model of communication. However, for my purposes here, describing simpler pictures as more effective because they *turn down the noise* inherent in communicating with highly detailed images diverts us from a more pressing question about visual communication. Namely, "how is it we can see the simpler pictures in the first place?" Answering this question might enable the creation of more communicative pictures. So, how is it that a visual system — the human eyes and brain — that has evolved over millennia through looking only upon the real world in all its detail, can understand, and as I will explain, sometimes even prefer, less than realistic pictures? In experiments intended to determine what kinds of pictures allow for easy identification of objects, or what kinds of pictures best allow the following of instructions, the most realistic picture has been persistently demonstrated not to be the most communicative. Line drawings perform better in this regard than photographs of the same things. It is an understatement to call these results surprising. If the human visual system has evolved among the real visual world, it should stand to reason that any means that can replicate that world accurately is the best means to communicate visual information to the reading or viewing audience. Photography springs most readily to mind if I may go back to Sontag's description of it as 'directly stencilled off the real'. Yet most of us *can* see and understand images that have been abstracted or stylised through drawings of various kinds; even those which have been reduced to simple stick figures. One might be tempted to pass this off as an issue of learned versus innate visual understandings; that people must learn to 'read' the non-realistic picture. However, understanding of abstracted and distilled pictures appears to preexist acculturation: infants, for instance, presented with two dots and a line in a facial arrangement spend more time viewing such a picture than they would a 'non-face' configuration of the same graphics. This suggests that such a picture is understood as representing a face (Morton & Johnson, 1991; Fantz, 1961). Perceptual psychologists since Helmholtz (1866) in the mid-19th century have understood that visual perception is related not just to objects in the real, visible world, but also to stimuli. For example, pressing on closed eyes can result in the perception of particular colours. Similarly, a flat, two dimensional surface that bears a picture can be a stimulus for the perception of an image. In light of this, I wish to explain some mechanisms of the human visual system that enable identification of less realistic pictures than those found away from the page in the real world. Further, I will try to demonstrate that these mechanisms allow that the visual system *prefers* less-than-realistic pictures.

The distant image

One reason we can see and understand less-real-than-real pictures might be that we have evolved having to deal with images presented to us at a distance. Such images are reduced in detail from the ideal required for recognition. An image is focused on to the retina, and converted into a language the brain can read — chains of electrical impulses (Gregory 1977). This retinal mosaic, however, is a finite number of components arranged across a finite area. The limited resolution that the retina provides means that only limited detail can ever be supplied to the brain. Limited resolution will affect the appearance of anything capable of being viewed over distance. If you look at a person across the room for example, no doubt they will be easy to recognise if you know them. If you don't know them, the fact of not knowing will be equally easy to establish. However, view that person from a distance of a few dozen metres and the ability to recognise them becomes fraught with error. Essentially, the main means of recognition, a good look at the face, is denied to you by the limited abilities of your eyes at this distance (Figure 8). The ideal viewing distance for human stereopsis (binocular vision) is six metres, or 20 feet in imperial measurement; hence 20/20 vision (Eden, 1978, p.205). Even with perfect 20/20 vision the information that your retinas can send to your brain becomes more and more limited beyond this distance. It is not that you see all the details of the face only smaller. Now, in fact, certain details have 'fallen away' altogether. The whites of the eyes will not be apparent, nor their colour, what may be visible is an area of darkness across the middle of the face suggesting the shadow of the brow as much as the presence of eyes. If the mouth is closed it will likely disappear as will the nose. The length of the chin or the depth of the forehead may be difficult to discern because these easily blend on your retinas with the blobs of colour where the neck and hair would be respectively. The image presented to you is less than the ideal needed for recognition: some of the details are literally missing because of the limited capacity of your retinas. In a sense this reality is less real, the image of the person at this distance is less representational than when they are in the room with you. The possibilities regarding who you are looking at are greater. Is this then, nature's form of the less representational picture?

Figure 8: Over distance, objects become more difficult to identify. Details of peoples' faces are not just smaller, but may not register at all on the viewer's retinas

In such a circumstance, you must call on other visual criteria for recognition. If you are quite familiar with the person you might recognise the cut or the colour of their clothes. Since a person may easily change these however, more indicative of their identity might be the way they move. You can best judge the identity of this person now, not on the recognition of their face but on how they move, upon their actions: In other words, by what they do. The way the coloured shapes on your retinas, that you recognise as the person's limbs, move around may tell you enough to narrow your hypotheses regarding this person. However, it is unlikely to narrow to the point where you can confidently say that this is one particular person. Instead you may be more concerned at the level of "does this person mean me harm?"; "are they behaving in a way I understand?"; and so on. The important matter to note is that you have begun to look at the person differently because you don't have the ideal information available for specific identification *via a good look at the face*. You may begin behaving differently because of the level of representation of the image; the image now means something different. At different distances we perceive a person differently. Up close we recognise them or recognise that we don't know them, we can read their facial expressions and better understand their mood and motives. If they are too far away for such recognition, other factors come into play, and when they are very far removed our decision making may be more in the order of 'is it a man or an animal? Is it an animal or a rock?'[1] These responses may go some way to explaining the workings of the 'realism continuum' more in terms of visual perception.

The silhouette

Another aspect of the visible world allows that the visual system might have evolved to understand less-real-than-real pictures: the silhouette. Depending on conditions of ambient light, the naturally occurring image of some person, creature or aspect of the landscape may appear as a more graphic shape than it would under conditions of, say, midday sunlight. Not only will this lighting diminish recognition of the specific person or thing, information regarding its three-dimensional shape will be lost to the eyes and must be made up where possible, presumably from memory. With regard to a hypothesis about a silhouetted person, this may not be too difficult. Stance, gait, profile, relative size of head to body and so on should give good clues as to age and sex and build, if not specific identity (Figure 9). The silhouette of an unfamiliar object will result in a greater range of hypotheses, and lengthen the odds of one of these being the correct one. A silhouette may indicate then what kind of object or person is in view but not easily allow us to solve what psychologists call the homogeneity problem, or which particular object or person is in view. The silhouette then is another way that images can be distilled down from reality, that is, have their realistic detail

---

1. Ekman, well-known for his study of emotion evidenced in facial expressions found that smiles can be seen from furthest away (300 feet) and with a briefer exposure than other emotional expressions (Ekman, 1985, p.149).

reduced, even in the real world. As a result, these kinds of images can cause a change in our response to the visual information from when we were presented with an image lit in such a way to provide easier recognition[2].

Figure 9: Human silhouettes lose specificity but, retain clues regarding gender and age.
Copyright Daisuke Fukushige, 2008

Simplest is best

So, even in nature there seem to be some images available to the eyes that communicate information without being typically 'realistic'. Things viewed from a distance and things viewed in silhouette provide a *less-real-than-real*

---

2. In *A Short History of the Shadow* (1997), Victor Stoichita explains that, historically, the silhouette has been regarded as a kind of hyperreal measure of the person or thing silhouetted.

version of what they would stand for at an ideal viewing distance in ideal light. However, this is a satisfactory explanation of how we link the abstraction to its realistic other only if the viewer knows what kinds of things s/he is looking at. Otherwise these 'less real' looking things would potentially be regarded as novel to the viewer, presenting, as they do, differently on the retina than would a closer and more ideally lit version of those same things. In fact, both of these possibilities, while perfectly logical are red herrings, although they may help provide part of the reason for the way the brain has evolved to deal with the information it gets from the eyes. Thinking carefully about the problem of viewing things under different lighting conditions or from different angles and distances leads to the realisation that any one thing is extremely unlikely to be viewed under exactly equal conditions twice. Even a slight change in the viewer's position will result in a different and unique image landing on the back of the eye. The human visual system therefore must have a 'degree of forgiveness'; some margin for error. The key issue to remember is that the eyes are doing one thing, the brain something altogether different with the same information. Thanks to a group of faculties of the visual system, under the name of 'perceptual constancies', the brain knows what the eye does not. These mental faculties override the purely visual sensations, and prevent us from mistaking novel presentations on the retina as novel objects because these faculties are unconcerned with specific information. In other words, these faculties concerned with constancy are mechanisms which tell all humans how to respond to their physical environment and tell the artist which aspects of the environment constitute the 'invariants' which were alluded to in the introduction to this book. These mechanisms are not present to acknowledge reality but rather to help us avoid being fooled by it. Which is to say that the visual system, even when abroad in the real world, is not merely accepting of what is presented on the retina, but in fact is measuring that presentation against what the brain knows of objects in the world. Gombrich uses a perfectly simple yet surprising example to explain:

> It is a fascinating exercise in illusionist representation to trace one's own head on the surface of [a steamed-up bathroom] mirror and to clear the area enclosed by the outline. For only when we have actually done this do we realize how small the image is which gives us the illusion of seeing ourselves 'face to face'. To be exact it must be precisely half the size of our head [...] since the mirror will always appear to be halfway between me and my reflection, the size on its surface will always be one half of the apparent size (Gombrich 2002: 5).

The visual detail of the real world is a difficult problem that needs to be solved. The image on the retina is not taken at face value: it is mediated and interpreted by the brain. How then, does the brain, or visual perception, decide that when the eyes present it with something it has never seen before, it may have seen that thing before but from another angle or at a different distance? Gombrich says:

> to probe the visible world we use the assumption that things are simple until they prove to be otherwise [...] A world in which all our expectations were constantly belied would be a lethal world. Now in looking for regularities, for

a framework or schema on which we can at least provisionally rely (though we may have to modify it for ever), the only strategy is to proceed from simple assumptions. (Gombrich 2002: 222)

Popper (1959) explains with disarming clarity that the mind is likely to select the simple proposition, not because it is most likely to be right but because it is the easiest to refute and therefore to modify (Figure 10).

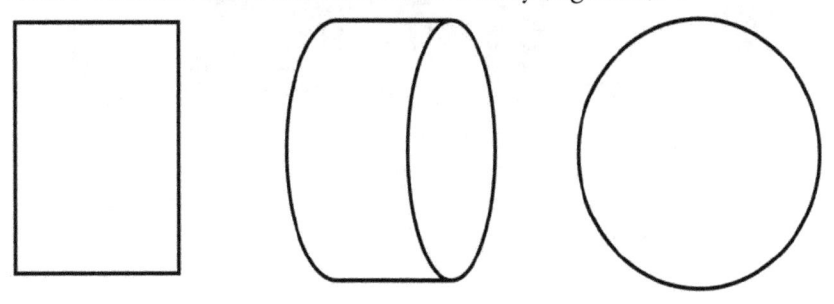

Figure 10: The simple object hypothesis is chosen by the human visual system because it is the most readily modified when the environment presents new clues. Medley after Zwimpfer

Psychologists place these mental mechanisms under the heading of 'perceptual constancy'. Shape, size and colour constancies are aspects of this mental faculty (Walsh and Kulikowski 1998: 492). Size constancy means that a given object is perceived as having the same size regardless of its distance from us. In other words, our knowledge of its size will override its presentation on the retina (as per Gombrich's face in the mirror experiment above).

Shape constancy means that an object is seen to have the same shape regardless of orientation. Thus we see things 'as they really are' and are not taken in by variations in the information presented to the retina (Figure 11).

Colour constancy means that an object is perceived as having the same colour in spite of changes in lighting conditions (Figure 12).

Other visual experiences which exhibit constancy include, but are not limited to, our perception of brightness, motion, and direction.

Figure 11: Even at marginally different angles, the retina must present the brain with unique views of objects. the brain must have a 'margin for error', or *shape constancy* in dealing with such visual information to avoid the assumption of a continuous stream of novel presentations

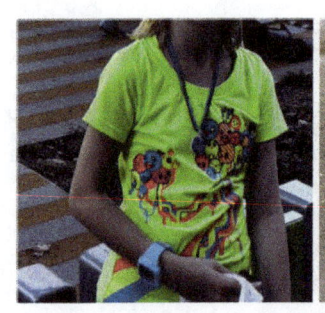

Figure 12: Lighting conditions change from room to room, and, in natural light, at different times of the day or as the subject moves from shadow to light. In this example, the green of the shirt is, to the eyes, much darker in shade, yet the brain understands this to be the same colour

Schema

This connection between the two visual versions of the same thing is what allows us to see the less realistic as having a relationship to the more realistic. Or rather, the less detailed can stand for the more detailed but perhaps in a more general way: the detailed version may be someone we recognize, a singular, specific person; the less detailed, distant version we may simply regard as 'a person'. The same would apply for the ideally lit figure and the silhouetted figure respectively. These faculties tell us that the real visual presentation of an object upon our retinas must be matched against existing information about these, or similar, objects in our memory in order for us to identify them. Implicit in this is that the knowledge already gained of the world exists in some kind of visual form. This form does not precisely match any 'real' visual version of such an object since the memory will contain a range of information from different viewpoints and under different lighting conditions. In fact 'form' itself is not really the right word since that suggests a given shape and size. This is why Gibson coined the term 'formless invariant' for these things that we recognise regardless of their distance from us or orientation to us. Again, in an attempt to keep this book accessible to graphic designers I think it is more helpful to use terms more familiar to the discipline. For this reason we will refer to these 'formless invariants' as schema. It may not be a common term in design parlance but for those practitioners and students who read the theory in the field it is more common than Gibson's terms. *Schema* and *schemata* occur frequently in Gombrich, Arnheim and Gregory, for example.

'Object-hypotheses' are our unconscious, best-guesses at what we are seeing. According to R.L. Gregory (1977), these are projected into external space and accepted as our most immediate reality. Gregory explains that an object-hypothesis cannot contain information on scale, distance or orientation because objects can be in an infinite number of positions in relation to the observer (1990, p.115). This implies that object-hypotheses must normally be scaled to fit the prevailing situation, by current sensory data. So we may suppose that they represent typical views and sizes, these being modified by available sensory information during perception. As Gombrich elucidates, "We look out into the world with the confidence that this thing out there will be more likely to change its place than its shape and that its illumination will vary more easily than its inherent colour" (2002, p.230). In other words, if the exact scale and colour of objects as they present on our retinas are not that vital to our understanding of the real world, and in fact these can be visual problems for the brain to overcome merely to function in the world, then their precision might not be so important in all pictures or in visual communication in general. So it is that schema, much-reduced in detail from the way things appear in the real world, can be a satisfactory visual explanation of aspects of the real world for the viewer. Schema are, in effect, what each of us are projecting into the external world to help us with our object-hypotheses. It is these schema that are, effectively, the lens through which each illustrator sees the world and presents it to us. Schema are the rules by which the artist has built his or her pictures.

In the field of illustration, comics artists, knowingly or otherwise, help solve these visual problems on behalf of their readers. In the world of comics, colour, for example, is less likely to change due to ambient lighting conditions than it might in the real world. Hergé said, "for a child, Tintin's jumper is blue, completely blue. Why should it be light blue on one side, and dark blue on the other?". For other comics artists a limited palette may be a result of simply being consistent with ink colours from frame to frame, but it is a colour consistency that is rare in nature and helps the reader establish, among other things, character identity. It is not a realistic use of colour but it communicates more directly than a realistic application of colour. As visual communicators we must ask ourselves what we want to communicate about an object or scene. Does the viewer of the picture need to know if it's a specific case or is the general case good enough? We now know that, because of these constancies, perfect accuracy is not so important to the human visual system but is often part of a difficult visual problem to be solved.

Visual closure

Perceptual constancy, as a set of psychological faculties, is enough to allow that the visual system understands less visible versions of things as being the same as ideally visible versions of those things. Along with 'closure' (Rauschenberger and Yantis 2001), the gestalt ability to group things, to assume patterns and finish in the mind objects half-glimpsed by the eyes, this understanding of abstracted pictures becomes an even more compelling argument. Closure is, Kepes tells us, "Certain latent inter-connections of points, lines, shapes, colours and values [which are] closed psychologically into bi-dimensional or tri-dimensional wholes' (Kepes 1944: 51), where the viewer will 'fill in the gaps'" (Figure 13). The faculty of closure does not have to reside in an ability to complete objects in the mind only when they are occluded. It also manifests itself in an ability to complete objects whose detail is only partly drawn, as if occluded but by some invisible artefact that merely 'removes' some details from the object being viewed. This would seem to allow that the 'invisible occlusion', which may exist in a drawing where detail is absent, be written off by the visual system as something not being focused upon. It is the object of attention that is important in order that the object-hypothesis problem may be solved.

VERY LONG CAT   **ONE SECOND LATER**

Figure 13: George Hardie's two-panel cat comic draws attention to visual closure. The second panel is designed to show that the closure provoked in the first is the wrong conclusion

Gestalt

Drawing a picture with the correct proportions but with little detail involved actually asks the reader to imagine the missing detail; to fill it in with their mind's eye. We've already seen that we can't help but make a face out of two dots and a line (E-mail sign-offs, such as <:(and :¬D are cases in point here and are an object of study in Chapter 5). This is the quintessence of Gestalt; seeing the whole from the parts.

The fact that this occurs in the human psyche means the designer, illustrator or artist can allow for the reader or viewer to complete very much of what's presented to him or her. The ability to group objects because of their similarity, closure and figural goodness are argued by gestaltists to be innately human abilities. That is, we do not need to learn these abilities, they pre-exist learning. Learning about new objects is facilitated by these abilities (Wertheimer, 1938). However, it is vital to note, as Lupton and Miller warn us, that these distilled pictures can only be perceived on a literal level. Any symbolic reference they make to larger concepts has to be agreed upon by convention and learned.

Together, these faculties of perceptual constancy and closure show that we can communicate visually with pictures that are less realistic than the things we see in the visible world. However, they do not prove that distillation — the act of reducing realism — is a more effective means by which to communicate or that humans may have a preference for the distilled image. Recent findings of the psychology of vision need to be examined to allow that the visual system might prefer less realism and less detail. The first of these will show that less realism is what the eye sees and the second will show that less realism is, rather perversely, what the brain prefers.

In order that our brains might better apply these models of perception—the constancies and closure—especially among all the distractions of the real world, there exists in the field of psychology conjecture about being able to focus eyes and brain on only a small part of what is before us:

> Focused visual attention resembles a spotlight or zoom lens. According to the zoom-lens model, visual attention is directed towards a given region in the visual field. [...] Much research has been carried out looking at what happens to unattended visual stimuli. The general view, supported by studies using fMRI, is that unattended stimuli receive a reasonable amount of processing but less than attended stimuli. (Eysenck, 2004, p.198)

It may be that this ability to process some aspects of the visual world more thoroughly than others allows for aspects of the visual world with less pertinent information in them to still be understood: that we are receiving these, perhaps not as accurately delineated objects and textures, but more as general shapes and colours. At the very least, this proposal allows that we can tune out aspects of the landscape: we can reduce the noise in the whole scene to focus on a specific aspect of it. In fact, it is only the central portion of the retina that can pick up detail anyway. Towards the outer limits, the older, less-evolved parts of the eye, unconcerned with colour or detail, send signals to the brain only upon the detection of movement: parts of the 'visible' world become visible only when they move. More on just what the eye takes in, later in this chapter; for now, this ability to tune out parts of the visible world would seem to reflect what may be done for a visual audience through illustration. The illustrator or designer making such a picture can make conscious decisions about what to remove and what to keep in order to communicate the core of the message. Of course, this may be achieved through photography, either through carefully staging the shoot, or 'in post' using the current image manipulation tools available to mask areas, crop pictures, amplify colours and so forth. But then doing all those things is doing precisely what I am advocating in this book: departing from realism. Typically though, as Peter Galassi, Chief Photography Curator at New York's Museum of Modern Art explains: "The photographic medium itself doesn't care what's important and what's not, so if you point it at something you think is important, it's going to register all the unimportant stuff around it with just the same precision and fullness" (Kirby, 2007).

Gestaltists have identified that we need to delineate before we can recognise. This is a crucial point to make: If noise—or reality captured somewhat indiscriminately in a photograph—hinders the delineation process then recognition is delayed. Distillation—the removal of noise before the sensation of the picture is received in the eye—might improve delineation and therefore speed recognition and understanding of a visual communication. The reduction of visual noise in turn allows changes in other visual qualities, such as an increase in contrast between figure and ground, which may also enhance easy recognition.

In other words, the visual system, in an attempt to focus on what it sees as the pertinent visual problem to be solved, can, with some concentration, 'tune out' the visual noise surrounding the object being gazed upon. This begs the question then, in graphic communication where we want the reader to respond in a particular way after they have deciphered the visual message, why not help solve the problem on his or her behalf by tuning out the noise rather than re-presenting the noise in the indiscriminate frame of a photograph? The designer sometimes wants to create visual puzzles for an audience to solve, perhaps in the hope that engaging with the picture helps retention of the message, or to provide the audience with a small sense of achievement upon the 'solution of the puzzle'. In either case, this understanding of what the brain applies to vision will help the designer.

The eyes and the brain have different tasks

Of course there exist further possibilities regarding the non-representative nature of nature. Despite existing of itself in all its infinite detail, the human organism simply does not take in the world in a representational manner. Or, having taken it in, the human mind might store it in codified and simplified ways that are not strictly representational. I will expand on this using reference to recent perceptual science discoveries about visual edge detection, rejection of large areas of flat colour, and the eye sending multiple different kinds of 'pictures' to the brain.

According to the perceptual constancies discussed, the eye and brain do different things. This is also what those very engaging visual puzzles and optical illusions show us, such as the Müller-Lyer and Sanders Illusions (Figures 14 and 15). These illusions show us some of the almost insignificant number of unlikely and very specific situations under which our otherwise reliable constancies fail us. According to recent studies on the eye, the images sent to the brain are not 'photographic' in the first place, or even very detailed at all. Without any optical trick being shown to the eye, the eye and the brain are 'seeing' differently anyway.

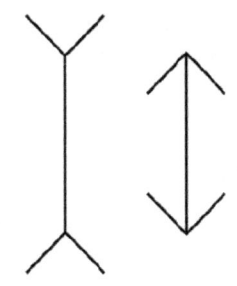

Figure 14: The Müller-Lyer Illusion suggests that the vertical line on the left is longer than the one on the right even though they describe the same visual angle on the retina

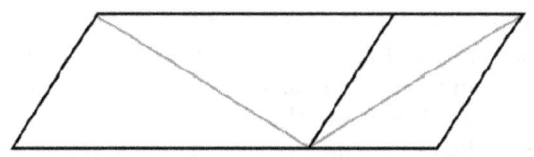

Figure 15: The Sanders Illusion uses angle to suggest that the grey line at the left is the longest. The grey lines are in fact the same length: the brain is over-riding the eye

What the eye sees

Certain brain cells are stimulated by certain patterns and by certain orientations of line, while other brain cells are stimulated by different orientations (Hubel and Wiesel, 1962, p.106). It seems also that the eye only gives very basic information to the brain and the brain fills in the rest of the detail (Roska and Werblin, 2001). The retina converts light into electrical impulses (the language of the brain). Some of these electrical messages are given only when the retina detects the edge of an object, others only when something is moving, others still only when something is seen to stop moving. What the eye sends to the brain, according to this research, are mere outlines of the visual world, sketchy impressions that make our vivid visual experience all the more amazing. Roska and Werblin provide evidence for between 10 and 12 output channels from the eye to the brain, each carrying a different stripped-down representation of the visual world.

In addition to their findings, a study published by the University of Texas at Austin (Geisler & Diehl, 2002) found that the visual system "is more sensitive to vertical and horizontal contours than to diagonal contours, perhaps reflecting the natural distribution of contour orientations" (p.421). There argument is that the visual system is best equipped to deal with things it is statistically more likely to find in the natural environment, but again, in broad terms, not on a level of intricate detail. Any picture which plays to these bigger, hard-wired visual themes is perhaps more likely to 'score a hit' on the visual system. If the eye really does work in this way, do distilled pictures better fit this model than the real world, giving the eye and brain, in effect a higher-impact version of reality? Pursuing illustrations

45

that remove some of the visual details found in the real world might help the visual communicator create scenes that can powerfully seize the attention of the eye and literally excite it.

What the brain understands

While the eye is reacting to the visions in front of it, and has a major role in delineating objects from background in order that the brain may understand its surroundings and have the organism respond appropriately, the brain is working to categorise those things the eye is delineating. As with the gestalt processes then, the mechanics of the eye are set up in such a way as to allow the brain to fill in the necessary information. The more the brain has learned, the better it fills the gaps, but the system that allows this seeing to happen is already in place in the same way that innate gestalt abilities pre-exist the ability to read yet afford this ability.

These recent discoveries only seem to confirm the generalist and abstract way the brain works in determining what belongs with what: Broader concepts such as shape and colour are paid most attention while less is given to fine detail. Detail seems to come into play close up, perhaps because by the time we have allowed something to approach us, or allowed ourselves to approach it, we have already determined, through these more generalist faculties, whether or not that thing is innocuous, or poses a threat or an opportunity.

Figure 16: Medley, *Life Boat*. Outlines, though non-existent in nature, are typical in comics and drawing in general. The appeal of these outlines might be because edge-detection in objects is a basic function of the eye

Caricature and the visual system

I have explored the idea of an image being less real than real as a function of distance. I have looked at the concept of perceptual constancies and closure as allowing the mind to complete a picture without all the pertinent information. Together, these concepts give us some strong evidence that the visual system can and does make meaning from less than realistic pictures; more accurately, from pictures that have been distilled or reduced somewhat from the detail of reality viewed under ideal conditions at ideal distances. The psychophysics of seeing which seem to suggest that the eyes send their information onto the brain as responses to only a limited number of stimuli provides further evidence that the brain is doing work that the eye does not, and that the eye is not even registering the kind of detail we associate with pictorial realism. None of these hypotheses however, explains a more bizarre faculty of the visual system: its ability to recognize people, not necessarily in a picture reduced in detail, but from a picture whose important details have been exaggerated. This kind of picture, best known as the province of the political cartoonist, is the caricature. Brennan defines caricature as:

> a graphical coding of facial features that seeks paradoxically to be more like a face than the face itself. It [...] amplifies perceptually significant information while reducing less relevant details. The resulting distortion satisfies the beholder's mental model of what is unique about a particular face. (Brennan 1985: 170)

To recognize an object, for example to distinguish a chair from a table, we must be able to map a potentially infinite set of images onto a single object representation: that is, we must solve what psychologists know as the 'object constancy problem'. However, to delineate one type of chair from another, or, more importantly, to delineate one face from another is a different problem for the visual system. Psychologist and face-recognition expert Gillian Rhodes explains how the visual system, in concert with cognitive apparatus in the mind, allows the brain to map new visual input against stored 'norms' (Rhodes 1996: 2–3). These norms exist for whole ranges of visual information and are expanded upon with further experience of the visual world. Where the new visual information differs from the norm, the mind appears to store these differences in a form exaggerated beyond their actual appearance. For example, if a person appears different from the norm because their head seems squarer than is normal ('normal' being defined by the different visual experience of each viewer) the brain will exaggerate this difference further still by making the head even more square in the stored memory of that person. (Figure 17)

Figure 17: Medley, *Robert Pattinson*. An effective caricature satisfies a viewer's understanding of what makes a face unique among all faces. It does so by exaggerating away from a norm those aspects unique to the face

In addition to this mental exaggeration of 'trends away from the norm', Rhodes explains that the visual system and the 'psychological landscape' to which it is linked are actually predisposed towards and on the lookout for extreme visual signals. She argues that:

> Stimuli that exaggerate some critical property of the natural stimulus, such as its size, contrast or number, often produce an enhanced response [...] This preference for extremes seems to be a fundamental feature of recognition systems, and one that imposes important constraints on the design of signals. (Rhodes 1996: 10)

Here Rhodes means 'design' in the sense of natural selection but the same might hold true for the human activity of design: exaggerated signals (those that do not naturally occur and are therefore not easily reproducible through photography) might actually communicate more immediately to a visual system predisposed to look for them: 'If drawings can be interpreted as externalizations of mental representations, then [...] those representations might themselves be caricatured. If so, then caricatures would be effective because they match the memory representations better than undistorted images!' (Rhodes 1996: 11). Annibale Carracci, the sixteenth-century artist, believed that, 'A good caricature, like every work of art, is more true to life than reality itself' (Geipel 1972: 56). As Gibson has said, a caricature may be faithful to those features of the man that distinguish him from all other men and thus may truly represent him in a higher sense of the term. It may correspond to him in the sense of being uniquely specific to him – more so than a projected drawing or photographic portrait would be. (Gibson 1971: 29). Whether a caricature can be more effective in recognition tasks and learning tasks has been the subject of debate for some decades. Tversky and Baratz (1985) found that photographs were better than line-drawn caricatures for "name recall, face recognition, and name-face verification reaction time". However, Gooch, Reinhard and Gooch (2002) maintain that the line-drawn caricature can perform better than photographs as long as the right method is used for generating the lines; a method that approximates shading through line width, among other techniques. In any case, the fact that this debate exists, that there is no immediately clear primacy between these two media, is in itself remarkable.

Real life is of course all about movement. While we are mostly concerned with 'static' pictures by way of explanation here, the movement consideration is still important. A good 'likeness' can be difficult to achieve through photography precisely because it takes a moment, let's say 1/100 of a second of someone's behaviour and captures it for all time. Meanwhile, if we know that person, our experience of that person (of all people in fact) in 'real-life' is of someone moving through time as well as space. We apprehend their expressions through time not as a split second removed from time. The camera can have trouble capturing the moment unless a very skilled portrait photographer is behind the lens. In light of this consideration regarding the difference between the caricatured drawing and the photograph of a specific person, it is perhaps not so surprising that some famous portrait photographers are actually caricaturists of sorts. Herb Ritts' portrait of actor Jack Nicholson, for example, exaggerates the famous grin through careful placement of a magnifying glass.

Specialist visual expertise can extend beyond faces and portraiture to recognition of any objects that may be discriminated by difference from a norm; in theory, any object can be caricatured. The criterion is that such a group of objects has a norm – real or imagined. To each of us these norms will be different. For those of us that work in specialist areas it might be easier than for others to conceive of a norm for, say, nuts and bolts, dresses, cars, buildings or landscapes. At Figure 18 is an example where the setting and the vehicle are caricatured. Where these differ from a 'normal' urban landscape (walls less straight than the rectilinearity of the illustrator's home environs) and a 'normal' car (the wheels of a Fiat 500 *are* smaller than average), these aspects have been exaggerated by the illustrator.

Figure 18: Olivier Kugler, Palermo detail. Any object may be caricatured if the artist can conceive of a norm for such an object. The differences between the object and its norm are then exaggerated away from the norm

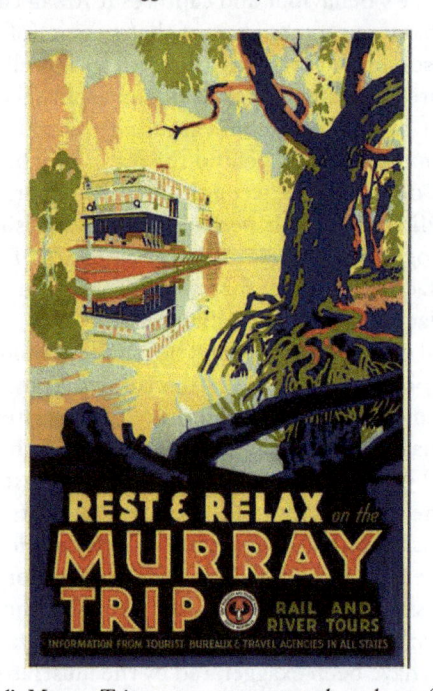

Figure 19: Goodchild's Murray Trip poster exaggerates the colour of the landscape while otherwise accurately drafting the proportions of the environment.
Courtesy South Australian Library

A visual ideal

The idea of an essential image that exists outside of either its corporeal embodiment or the realistic capture of that embodiment through photographic means is redolent of Plato: representative imagery, the realistic picture, might merely be a shadow on the wall of a cave while its essence lies elsewhere. For our purposes here that essence resides in the human mind. As Gregory suggests, it is the object-hypothesis that the artist communicates with, using typical views drawn from somewhere within. He argues that the object-hypothesis must then come from memory. Those slight differences in the images of things within the same class (for example, within the class of human faces) that enable this object-hypothesis may be stored as caricature. With an awareness of the mind's faculty for caricature, the designer might then caricaturise or anticaricaturise (drive the differences back towards the norm rather than away) the features of the person, or object, towards a desired effect.

The importance of synaesthesia in visual communication

All of the above are strictly visual processes and assume that vision is clearly delineated from the other senses. Other theorists talk about body-felt experience of vision. What does that mean and how is it significant to understanding pictures? It means that our sense of the visual is impacted upon by our other senses; rather than each sense being discretely contained, they spill over into one another. The circle might appear a more relaxing shape to look upon than the triangle for example, because the circle has no sharp corners on which, in the physical world, we might catch ourselves. The jagged line looks dangerous and unpleasant compared to a gently curving arc for the same reasons. To some extent, these physical attributes seem to stand beyond culturally specific (linguistically, experientially or temporarily defined) interpretation. Ramachandran and Hubbard, in *Synaesthesia: A window into perception, thought and language,* surveyed people of both English and Tamil language backgrounds to test what is known as the 'Bouba/Kiki effect':

> If you show fig. [20] (left and right) to people and say 'In Martian language, one of these two figures is a "bouba" and the other is a "kiki", try to guess which is which', 95% of people pick the left as kiki and the right as bouba, even though they have never seen these stimuli before. The reason is that the sharp changes in visual direction of the lines in the left-hand figure mimics the sharp phonemic inflections of the sound kiki, as well as the sharp inflection of the tongue on the palate. The bouba/kiki example provides our first vital clue for understanding the origins of proto-language, for it suggests that there may be natural constraints on the ways in which sounds are mapped on to objects. Second, we propose the existence of a kind of sensory-to-motor synaesthesia,

which may have played a pivotal role in the evolution of language. A familiar example of this is dance, where the rhythm of movements synaesthetically mimics the auditory rhythm. (2001b, p.19)

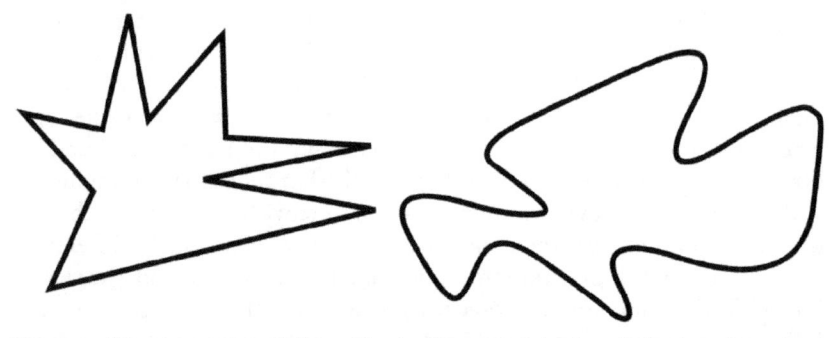

Figure 20: "Demonstration of kiki and bouba. Because of the sharp inflection of the visual shape, subjects tend to map the name kiki onto the figure on the left, while the rounded contours of the figure on the right make it more like the rounded auditory inflection of bouba." from Ramachandran, V.S. & Hubbard, E.M. (2001b)

Ramachandran and Hubbard are unconcerned specifically with distilled imagery, but these experiments which play with the demarcation of senses might suggest that distilled pictures can more easily cross this border from the visual sense into the other senses. McCloud seems to grasp this also when he explains that it is much easier for a cartoon drawing to enter the realm of ideas than it is for a highly representational image (1993, pp.24-59).

In summary

Given that a designer is often communicating to a wide audience (economic imperatives most often dictate that the designer's client is trying to reach as wide an audience as possible to inform and persuade about a product, service or event) s/he needs to be especially adept at the object constancy problem, specifically what attributes of the object make it different to all other objects. To help solve the object constancy problem on behalf of his or her audience, the designer should be adept at showing typical objects of that class from pertinent angles (or describing to an illustrator the requirements of the task). However, once a designer hones in on the type of picture or pictures to use in a particular promotion, a decision should be made about what particular example of that class of things to portray. According to Rosch (1978) category members closest to the prototype are easiest to learn, more rapidly identified and more likely to be retrieved. The designer must decide whether the object will be typical or atypical depending on the nature of the communication. If the example required is atypical, the designer must be aware also, consciously or by instinct, of the *homogeneity* problem. It is my conviction that a conscious awareness of the problem is best since, in the aim of this book, design is about decision making for effective communication, and less about artistic expression. Caricature, as a process of picture making would seem to be an appropriate and useful skill to obtain for visually solving this problem. In Chapter 5 of this book I use particular exemplars, related to these different psychological faculties, that illustrate the points so far discussed.

In closing this examination of the psychology of seeing, it's clear that we are able to see things presented to us in less than realistic ways. Not only does the human visual system relate these to real things, it might actually prefer these distilled versions and possibly store them better in memory because they are already put into the form in which the memory stores them. Furthermore, it may be that photography is not the best means for capturing realistic and specific things, since caricature seems to have the potential to do this better in terms of viewer retention.

Returning to the realism continuum model, it helps us to solve the homogeneity problem at its more specific or realistic end (the difference between Tom Dick and Harry, or even between an Eames chair and a Breuer chair). At the other end of the scale, the less real end, it helps the visual communicator sort out the object constancy problem; is this a man or a dog, a chair or a table? Fussel and Haaland's (1978) Nepalese study results, discussed previously, might even suggest the following order as a *recognition continuum* in place of the realism continuum: beginning with the most easily recogniseable the order would seem to be: line drawing with shading and internal detail; photograph with background removed; line drawing; silhouette; photograph; stylised drawing. As Shaw (1969) found, attempting to communicate with too realistic a picture raises its own problems: "the degree of identification becomes too specific" (p.7). Shaw showed that a tendency already exists for the less graphically literate to seek specificity in even non-photographic depictions of humans. It seems to me that where photography is used and a specific person is captured, and specificity of that character is *not* the intention of the communication, this problem of seeking specificity will only be exacerbated. The detailed line drawing in Fussel and Haaland may owe its communicative success to being in a kind of 'sweet spot' for the human visual system as a drawing that can solve both the object constancy and the homogeneity tasks. According to Gooch, Reinhard and Gooch, (2002) the processing that takes place in the early stages of human vision appears to produce imagery that resembles line drawings. Perhaps these pictures do some of the work of the human visual system prior to perception, boosting cognition. For some particular communication problems at least, this kind of depiction may be the ideal between realism and distillation.

In any case, having examined some of the ways in which the mind is trying to 'solve the problem of realism' rather than to take it for granted, I want to ask why graphic design has been so enamoured of the realistic picture. In the next chapter I will explore some of the reasons for photography's primacy in the field of graphic design. None of these reasons has anything to do with the psychology of seeing.

Chapter 3
A History of the Picture in Graphic Design

Given that graphic design is regarded as having begun with the art poster (Heller, 1999), and the art poster was executed using pen and brush, and reproduced via lithography or serigraphy, why should photography gain a foothold in this field and later turn it into a stranglehold? If a general statement can be made about graphic design that encompasses the various political and economic drivers of it, then it is that its makers want to reach an audience of some size to communicate a message. In order to get that message out to more than one audience member at a time, replication is a necessity. For this reason, painting is not an appropriate medium but lithography is since it allows for replication of a picture. Lautrec, the Beggarstaffs, Lucien Bernhard and other pioneers of the poster replicated their drawn and painted images using lithography. Photography allowed this replication to continue but its mechanistic capture of images also cut short the time taken to make the initial picture.

The Bauhaus is not the hermetically sealed birthplace of mechanistic design but merely one of several nodes in Europe where it first appeared. Two further nodes are vital to mention: The Dutch and the Russian. From the Dutch the Bauhaus, and ultimately the Swiss derived their devotion to geometry. The geometric approach is clearest in the work of the Dutch De Stijl movement and was brought to the Bauhaus in person by De Stijl supremo, Theo Van Doesburg. For De Stijl, geometry and a reliance on primary colours was a means to express the dynamic yet balanced, natural forces underlying the universe. It is this almost platonic quest for the essence of form that found its ultimate expression in the International Styles of architecture (through Mies van der Rohe's buildings) and graphic design (in the work of the Neue Schweizer Grafik, also referred to as 'The International Typographic Style'). For the Bauhaus, the significance of the geometric approach to graphic design lay in its affinity to machine replication and a technical aesthetic: "trained in the language of form, Bauhaus designers set about developing prototypes for the mass-production of definitive, standard forms for the objects of everyday life, basing their approach on the premise that people's practical needs are largely identical" (Rowland, 1990, p.12).

From the Russian constructivists came the Bauhaus devotion to photography. Photomontage was brought to the Bauhaus by Hungarian, Laszlo Maholy-Nagy, himself a constructivist typographer and photographer. The constructivists had embraced photography because they "rejected the idea of a unique work of art as belonging to the old bourgeois society [...] the mechanical production of images through photography fitted their ideology" (Hollis, p46). The Russian photographic work is famously embodied in El Lissitsky and Rodchenko:

> they were exhibiting some of the characteristics of the International Style. What became the common language of graphic design thirty years later included the emphasis on rectangularity and on white space as part of the design, an exclusive use of sans serif typefaces and photography rather than drawn illustration. (Hollis, p.48)

Photography had long been a consuming interest at the Bauhaus, and it had been fuelled by the presence of Moholy-Nagy and his wife Lucia, who were outstanding and inventive photographers (Rowland, 1990). Maholy-Nagy was especially focused on the integration of typography and photography in what he termed 'Typofoto' communications. Bayer and others further applied these principles in advertising design, incorporating "imaginative use of photography. [...] This work had an enormous influence on the German advertising industry, and its importance was immediately recognized. In 1927, for instance, the Association of German Advertising Specialists held its training course at the Dessau Bauhaus" (Rowland, 1990, p.126).

So it seems that the spread of photography as a means of capturing image for communication design was carried out into the world, not only by the students of the Bauhaus, but by the commercial mainstream of practising designers in the advertising industry. In addition, this influence soon became a global one with the "forced emigration of progressive designers from Germany" under the rule of the Nazis (p.127). Many of these designers found their way into the British and American mainstreams of advertising design while others, such as Moholy-Nagy worked in London (in documentary film-making) and went on to establish courses in eminent design schools in the U.S., such as the 'New Bauhaus' in Chicago. It is possible also to find reference to this spread of photography for design outside of the more well-known progression from Germany to the U.S. For example in Wlassikoff's French perspective on the history of graphic design:

> The technique of photomontage, which was initially practiced only by avant-garde artists, developed in the USSR in the late 1920s. It was encouraged by the propaganda services [...] The extremely official L'URSS en construction magazine, distributed around the world in several languages, was one of the main proponents of this type of design, produced by such artists as Lissitsky, Kloutsis, and Trochine. (2005, p.123).

This global distribution allowed not only the dissemination of a striking use of photography but also meant that in each of the countries it reached, it was adopted as a style to speak in a relevant way to local audiences.

A revisitation of constructivist principles, including photomontage, occurred with the deconstructionists half a century later, and I will examine shortly where and why this happened. For my purposes here, it is important to note these polar, contradictory attractors in graphic design. They pull in one direction towards the minimalism, distillation and generality inherent in the use of the grid and geometry as an organizing principle, and, in the opposite direction, towards the specificity and detail inherent in the photograph.

The work of Lucien Bernhard and his colleague, Hans Rudi Erdt at Hollerbaum and Schmidt, that predates the Bauhaus, is among the few pieces that show a concerted push towards distillation in pictures. Graphic design historian, Meggs, puts this down to spur-of-the-moment instinct from Bernhard rather than any manifestation of theory or technical approach:

> This self-taught young artist probably did not realize it at the time, but he had moved graphic communications one step further in the simplification and reduction of naturalism into a visual language of shape and sign. Toulouse-Lautrec had started the process and the Beggerstaffs had continued it, but Bernhard established the approach to the poster of using flat colour shapes, the product name, and product image. (2006, p.270)

Again, graphic design's development appears reactionary. Heller (2000) sees Bernhard's success as a reaction to the visual excesses of the Art Nouveau designers:

> Industrialization, the growth of the cities, the increase of vehicular traffic, and the fast pace of every-day life required that advertisers compete for attention as never before. Visual complexity no longer worked. Passersby moved much too quickly to appreciate the levels of craft and symbolism in elaborate art nouveau compositions. (p.139)

Certainly, after Bernhard emigrated to the US in 1923, noone seems to have specifically taken up where he left off. His avenue of visual exploration was turned into a cul-de-sac by the adoption of photography at the Bauhaus.

The Neutral Swiss: Modernism falters through prescription of photography

In the west, most of the few canonical texts we have devoted to graphic design education were penned by advocates of Die Neue Schweizer Grafik. This has had the function of limiting possibilities for design educators since because these authors make absolute claims about, not just type and grid, but the superior efficacy of photography in graphic design. As Hollis explains in his *Graphic Design a Concise History,* "Modernism in Switzerland became a crusade in the years following the Second World War. Its assumptions became matters of faith" (1994, p.130). Given that the central credo of the Swiss Typographers is to effectively communicate the client's message in a clear and unbiased fashion, these designers fall demonstrably short of their own lofty aims. Die Neue Schweizer Grafik is the natural progression from the Bauhaus. While certain celebrated designers and typographers, Jan Tschichold, among them, himself formerly of the Bauhaus, maintained that graphic design had moved on from the Bauhaus, a movement developed in post-war Switzerland and Germany that clung to certain of the Bauhaus' typographic principles, not least because some of its principle practitioners had been Bauhaus students. In Germany, Otl Aicher founded the Ulm design school with Max Bill (an ex-Bauhaus student and Swiss Typographer). According to Aicher's biographer, Marcus Rathgeb (2006), the invitation to Bill to head the school was at least in part to get the New Bauhaus (Chicago) on side and to encourage U.S. funding for the school. At least some of the school's approach was designed to appease its potential sponsors, the ex-Bauhaus staff now ensconced at the Chicago Institute. From Ulm the formulaic use of sans-serif type, gridded layouts and photographic imagery spread throughout the western world, and even into the design schools of South America.

> The Hochschule fur Gestaltung in Ulm, Germany, greatly influenced the propagation of design education and design discourse in Latin America during the 1960s. At that time, the creation of the first institutions for design education proliferated in Latin American countries as they reoriented themselves toward a policy of import substitution and industrial development. The German school was the only institution that offered, within those countries' contextual conditions, an operative, concrete answer to the challenges of industrialization. In addition, it championed the insertion of design into the industrial process while rejecting all artistic or decorative speculations about design activity. (Fernandez, 2006, p.3)

The proponents of the Swiss School made claims regarding the superiority of photography as a means of effective graphic communication. Josef Müller-Brockmann, one of the key figures of Swiss Typography, in his graphic design text-book, *The Graphic Artist and his Design Problems,* wrote:

photography provides an objective picture of material reality and thus conveys an impression of authenticity. It requires no effort to understand its message. Where photography is concerned, the modern publicity expert need not hesitate to exploit all its different modes of expression in order to influence opinion. When the camera records a situation, it furnishes objective information on an event, whether it shows a total picture or only a detail. (1983, p.27)

We can not be sure what Müller-Brockmann meant by 'all its different modes of expression'. He may, judging by his experiments of 'painting with light' and with photograms, have been referring to atypical uses of photography, but in so doing he would be at odds with his own statement about photography furnishing objective information on an event, which seems to refer to photography's documentary capabilities. Many of the tone drop out and double-exposure experiments of the Swiss witness a struggle with this prescriptive notion of photography for all graphic design imagery. Some of the Swiss practitioners appear to be exploring ways to remove photography from the grasp of realism in order to suggest something more symbolic, more illustrative. However, not content with elevating photography, Müller-Brockmann felt it necessary to denigrate illustration:

comparison will show that the drawing is a subjective expression of the artist's mind and is restricted to the moment of its creation. It depicts an object or a theme as he experienced it at a specific moment whereas photography shows what the camera could objectively record when the shot was taken. The photographer simply points the lens of his camera at whatever it is he wants to photograph. The drawing conveys to us the feeling of the artist whereas the camera reproduces solely material facts and events. (p.27)

Lupton and Miller give this comparison between illustration and photography, specifically, the rise of photography in the history of design, more consideration:

By the 50s, photography had come to dominate the promotion of food, furniture, and housewares, areas where the copious detail provided by the camera was invaluable. Some products, however, benefitted from more interpretive merchandising. Fashion and pharmaceuticals were among those industries that favoured illustration. In the case of medical products, drawing was considered more appropriate than photography, for it offered a veiled rather than literal depiction of illness. Pharmaceutical advertising was directed at medical professionals, an upper-middle-class group that the ad industry regarded as receptive to the 'cultured' appeal of artistic illustration. (1999, p.78)

Even Andy Warhol produced illustrations for several pharmaceutical companies during the 50s, including CIBA-GEIGY and Upjohn, both known for their progressive design. While Lupton and Miller ably substantiate the advertising industry's preference for illustration in particular contexts, this approach was by no means universal. Müller-Brockmann, in his crusade for photography, applied it ubiquitously in his pharmaceutical advertising (also for Geigy). Lupton and Miller suggest that photography has ultimately triumphed as the designer's picture medium of choice: "While illustration continued to be an important profession within graphic design, Warhol might have sensed photography's encroachment, and surely he sensed its power" (p.88).

The vectors by which this graphic aesthetic reached all corners of the Earth are worth mapping out. The Swiss Style may have had some global success in and of itself via the ubiquity of chemical and pharmaceutical products—The visual stylings of Geigy A.G. were disseminated through the company's subsidiaries in the US and the UK, and through their publicity departments in Spain, Italy, Canada and Australia (Janser & Junod, 2009). To further consolidate this relationship between commercial work and education as it pertained to pharmaceutical graphics, several of the designers at Geigy returned to the Basel School of Design to teach. The school itself is central in the history of 20th Century communication design. In addition, as if providing early career opportunities to design graduates and providing teachers back to the School of Design was not enough to inculcate a style into the growing discipline of graphic design, Geigy also manufactured many of the printing and reprographic chemicals necessary for design production—But, it was the Swiss Style's consolidation of the Bauhaus principles laid down decades before, and the network of design schools and studios set up by Bauhaus teachers throughout the world that guaranteed a sanguine international uptake of the Swiss graphic themes (Medley, 2009).

Other important design texts have joined the Swiss canon of graphic design 'must-reads'. Despite a less didactic approach than the Swiss school, these newer texts still suffer from the bias towards type at the expense of pictures. Even recent works that specifically seek to address the relationship between text and image, fall short of exploring the possibilities of illustration by assuming, on behalf of their audience, a reliance on photography to express the picture aspects of design: "Complexity adds to the time needed to investigate and interpret a work, regulated by each viewer's level of experience. For intricacy to transcend entanglement, designers must embrace the creative potential of photo-typographic space" (Skolos & Wedell, 2006, p.10).

The texts that disseminate the message of graphic design through to subsequent generations of graphic designers are either by the early modernists, the Swiss typographic school, or contemporary modernists very much influenced by their predecessors. Their approach to typography may vary slightly but their reliance on photography with regard to image borders on absolute. This unquestioning reliance on photography is compounded by various of the early key texts on visual literacy which had a camera-centric focus. This typo-photo-centric approach may well be symptomatic of a design education where whole courses are spent honing design students' typographical skills, but little emphasis seems to be placed on other visual literacies. In my own narrow experience of half a dozen universities, these pictorial 'instincts' are essentially the qualities assessed by design academics during admission interview for design courses, and they are not conceived of as a set of skills that may be taught or learned like typography. Indeed, the pictorial is largely left to the instincts of the individual student. Evidence for this attitude towards pictures also exists in the big-name design annuals, which aim to feature the best designs from around the world yet offer no explanation of judges' criteria for choosing individual pieces for inclusion.

During the 1950s and 60s, at the height of Die Neue Schweizer Grafik, but over in the U.S., there were various picture treatments evident. Illustration was clearly held in some regard, at least its prevalence and the rates paid to 'name illustrators' would suggest so, though no-one seems to have articulated its specific strengths during this period. Lupton and Miller (1999) see its prominence then as due to its status: it was used to advertise high-class goods because of an obvious association with the visual arts: it looked more like painting than photography did, and photography was yet to be accepted as an art form in and of itself. But this was all soon to change as publicity in the U.S. began to adopt (or pervert, depending on which critic one reads) European Internationalism. In Switzerland no such distinction between high and low advertising had existed: the same designer could easily work on the latest breakfast snack or the state opera. Indeed this seems in accord with the continuation of the stated aims of the Bauhaus, to democratise visual communication. In any case, "the rise of the camera and the diminishing prestige of hand-drawn illustration" (Lupton & Miller, p.88), in part due to photographers now being able to execute a 'signature style', ensured that photography also began to become apparent in graphic design in the States. At the same time, the head-quarters of the Swiss pharmaceutical and chemical giants, chief patrons of the International Style of sans serif type and photography, began to rein in the regionally particular designs of their products in favour of global consistency (Medley, 2009). The struggle of illustrators in the face of the all-conquering photograph would not have been helped by the increasing adoption of Swiss modernist methods by the American advertising industry either. American design icon, Paul Rand, for example, worked with Josef Müller-Brockmann to develop the IBM corporate identity, going so far as to present workshops to IBM staff on what constituted effective visual communication (Müller, 2001, p.213).

Deconstructionist graphics

The graphic design approach that significantly challenged the Neue Schweizer Grafik was the Deconstructionist design of the late 1980s and early 1990s. In these designs, as with post-modernism in architecture and the arts, historical references were plundered, removed from their contexts and put to work in new messages. Aesthetically speaking though, this loose movement of design, owes a good deal to the Russian constructivists (Figure 21). Unlike the constructivists, or the Swiss for that matter, designers that pursued a deconstructive path were reluctant to discuss direct communication of a message, citing instead the subjectivity of the author and the audience, or poststructuralist principles regarding the failings of communication; that there can be no consensus regarding the meaning of a piece of design:

> In the 1990s, the idea that visual communication tends to be too prescriptive was a constant refrain among younger designers. Many rejected the idea that it was their job to transmit a direct, unambiguous message [...] They argued that

their own screen-fed generation was able to handle messages of much greater complexity. Using computers, they blitzed their peer group with overloaded patchworks of text and image to filter and process. Let the viewer decide what it all meant.' (Poynor, 2001, p.78)

A reaction against the Swiss reliance on grids and sans serif type saw the deconstructionists throw up explosive looking layouts like paint splashed on to a canvas. Recurring themes included computer glitches; repetitively cut, pasted and distressed type, and densely overlaid graphics in order to reveal the 'made' nature of these pieces, and perhaps, by extension, the made nature of all graphic design. The implication being that, far from providing a conduit for the client, the designer is, him or herself, an author of the message (Figure 22). Far from Lars Müller's (2000) criticism that the reader's "eye is wearied by lack of content, aesthetically veiled" and that this approach did little more than "encourage affective consumerism" deconstructionism was, if only initially, an attempt to break away from a modernism that had become the herald of the corporate world; the spent force of the Neue Schweizer Grafik. As this new 'style' too began to be subsumed, inevitably, into the commercial realm, what began as a refreshingly honest approach to graphic design can easily be criticised on the following grounds: the designer abrogated responsibility for the appropriateness, or otherwise, of the design to the client who chose it (since the designer was essentially repeating his or her own style with each piece). The client, presumably the less visually literate of the two parties, had decided the design approach for the message by choosing the designer. In short, the client, acting through, or in effect as, an art director, was making the principle design decisions.

DECONSTRUCTIONIST GRAPHICS

Figure 21: Phedra theatre poster by Dirk Behage, Pierre Bernard and Fokke Draaijer, France 1991. This work shows the clear lineage to the Russian constructivists typical of early deconstructionist work, through its colour and typographic palette and its reliance on photography and photomontage

63

Figure 22: A common and important theme in deconstruction is the revelation of the process through which the design is constructed. In this case, Nick Bell's illustration for the IBM annual review, 1991, shows the ease with which images are copied and pasted using the newly acquired digital technology

Importantly for my purposes here, the deconstructionists' rejection of credo and didacticism resulted in an absence of teaching materials. Few post-modernists have authored prescriptions for effective visual communication that answer the problems posed by the International Style (the aforementioned, Skolos & Wedell's, *Type, Image, Message* being an exception). On the contrary, despite their rejection of the Swiss grid and the mythic neutrality of modernist design, the post-modernists clung to photography as the principle means of representing the visual world. From the deconstructionists we are left with a series of 'eye-candy' books, held together, more or less, by their style and the editors' understanding of the theory behind the work (as in the aforementioned, *Typography Now*). Regardless of what these designers rejected from the Swiss or the Bauhaus, their repeated homage to the Russian avant-garde shows that what they have not rejected is photography as the principle medium for expressing image in graphic design. It may be that the early deconstructionists, those knowingly adopting the techniques of the constructivists, were attempting to rediscover the fabled democratising aspects of photography that their Russian predecessors had so believed in; to return to an idealist modernist mode, pre-Paul Rand (who, as Rick Poynor argues, 'stripped modernism of its ideological purpose in the United States and realigned it with corporate interests'). It is no coincidence that Paul Rand, in his essay From Cassandre to Chaos (1991), joined the heated debate on the side of the old versus the new avant-garde of graphic design, calling the work of the deconstructionists, 'indecipherable'. In a political sense at least the deconstructionist designers were reflecting the ethics of the Bauhaus, especially Lazslo Maholy-Nagy's belief that man, not the product, is the end in view.

As I stated in my introduction, graphic designs generally consist of combinations of the two elements, type and picture. It is patently clear, especially from an examination of the aforementioned textbooks, that, whether Modernist or Post-modernist, the predisposition of design theorists, educators and professionals, is to concern themselves primarily with type. Indeed, the term 'typography' has been largely interchangeable with 'graphic design' since the Bauhaus. Rarely has discussion focused upon the choice of picture in graphic design: it is the designer's choice of type and their layout of that type that is regarded as of fundamental importance. While it may seem churlish to criticize the prescriptions of a school of thought most famous for its mid-century output, the approach of the Swiss is perpetuated into this century, noteably through Bosshard (2000), Samara (2002) and Elam (2004).

Zeitgeist: why deconstruction in 1980s?

Timothy Samara, in *Making and Breaking the Grid*, (2002) makes the case for the introduction of digital technology, specifically the Apple Computer as the designer's tool, as the catalyst for the explosion of deconstruction in the 1980s. An embrace of earlier technologies enabled the proliferation of gridded design in the 1920s according to Samara:

> Just as the use of grids in modern design practice grew from the developments in technology, aesthetic thought, and industrialization, the use of alternate, intuitive methods of composition—prevalent in current design practice—grew from these same influences. (p.112)

Of course, in and of itself, the computer as a supremely logical machine should in fact allow a more precise refinement of, and attachment to a typographic grid, the supremely logical system for layout. It is the social zeitgeist suggested by this profound change in technology and technique which actually led to the rejection of the grid, and a re-appraisal of the constructivist and modernist work that had arrived at the dawn of the previous machine age in the 1920s. In spite of the many critiques levelled against them, deconstructionist designers were essentially reworking Da Da, De Stijl and Constructivist methods from the early 20s. Neville Brody made a name for himself by reworking, and with heavy irony, the pure modernist aesthetic of the Bauhaus and the Swiss School, "to draw a parallel between the social climate of the 1930s and the 1980s" (Poynor, 1991, p.11).

These past movements and approaches to design were revisited knowingly, ironically and sometimes cynically or with humour but rarely with a sense of building on sound theoretical foundations. As Rick Poynor observed in *Typography Now* as the fledgling Deconstructionists attempted to take flight in 1991: "Although the idea of deconstruction is gaining ground among designers in the U.S., and enjoys some currency in Europe where it originated, few typographers would feel sufficiently confident of the theoretical basis of the term to describe themselves as deconstructionists" (p.14). This uncertainty extended to a lack of exploration of visual techniques: type and its placement was clearly—as evidenced in any number of examples from the 1990s—the principle focus of these designers. This is largely because in typography there were defined boundaries against which to push. Beyond this the Deconstructionists explored what the technology enabled in terms of photographic manipulation, but their questioning of the tenets of the Swiss never extended as far as questioning the Swiss reliance on photography. In the end, it is the differences in layout and typography, and not the pictorial elements that show the clearest separation between the adherents of the grid and the rejectors of the grid.

In its infancy, deconstruction was applied to the promotion of events, gallery openings, exhibitions, and plays directed and produced by like minded individuals. In no way was it a mainstream approach to visual communication. While the new deconstructionist aesthetic was revolutionary, both in the sense that it replaced the old guard, and in the sense that it was an old approach coming around again, it ultimately did little to shake the status quo of visual communication. If anything it led to an accelerated generation of visual surfaces at the expense of resonant content and form. Because of its startling look, this style all too easily became recognised for its surface. Because the designers themselves, those few who really understood its politics, declared their authorship of each piece—essentially to own up honestly that all communication has an author—these people were easily singled out as artists. No quantum leap is required from this concept to the one of celebrity, a concept that the mainstream can easily deal with. Soon enough, several of these graphic designers, in something of a first for design history, became famous beyond the immediate circle of their discipline: "Neville Brody and David Carson achieved something that in graphic design and typography was nonexistent before them and that was superstar status" (Walters, "Gerard Unger", 2001).

Deconstructionist design is the antecedent to the contemporary visualities in design. It is the last semi-homogenous aesthetic movement of, if not theoretical approach to, graphic design before the onset of our current cornucopia of visual approaches. Why did these other aesthetics and approaches follow deconstruction? I will attempt to answer this question in terms of these contemporary graphics being political reactions to the previous design movement.

Pictures in contemporary design

As I have mentioned above with regard to the deconstructionist reaction to the grid, the push for change was squarely against the assumed rules of typography, not against the prescriptions the Swiss had laid down for design's pictorial content. While graphic design and typography remain more or less interchangeable terms, I want to examine the contemporary expressions of graphic design that have flourished in the aftermath of deconstruction that are not concerned specifically with type, but rather show an unprecedented emphasis on pictures. The fields of design that have burgeoned as never before are information design and illustration. Neither of these could justifiably be described as 'typography'. These forms of graphic expression are also especially worthy of note in this book as neither uses photography as its primary imagery nor particularly strives for pictorial realism. These two graphic design fields have different purposes, but each has grown as a result of what happened to graphic design in the 1990s, rather than as an outcome of some new-found visual literacy. Where the Neue Schweizer Grafik was deemed a spent force by the Deconstructionists, because of its formulaic sameness or its didactic message, the explosive appearance of the deconstructionist pieces made them easy to co-opt as an exciting new style through which to 'sell more units':

> The advertising agencies did not dilute the message by making their own pale copies, as they had with Neville Brody's work in the mid-1980s. They bought the product direct from the source. Nike's U.S. Agency, Wieden & Kennedy, was one of the first to set a premium on fashionable type by calling in Brody himself to help sell training shoes in 1988 [...] Robert Nakata, A Cranbrook Academy of Art-educated typographer known for boldly experimental projects at Studio Dumbar, left the Hague-based company to join Wieden & Kennedy's Amsterdam office where he has created print campaigns for Nike and Microsoft. (Poynor, 1998, p.10)

Claudia Mereis, in her foreword to *Illusive 1: Contemporary illustration and its context*, has specifically talked about illustration's rise in the early 2000s as a reaction to what came immediately before: "After the euphoria of the digital age there is a vociferous demand for more personal quality and poetry. Functionality and coolness no longer seem worth striving for, people are looking for honest human communication, with rough edges and corners. So we can also see a return to analogue and manual techniques in contemporary illustration" (2005, p.3). I will examine below how I believe the growth in the use of illustration has been organically seeded by Deconstruction. Meanwhile, Richard Saul Wurman has described the concurrent and sudden interest in information design (at the beginning of the new millennium) as follows: "when I came up with the concept and the name information architecture in 1975, I thought everyone would join in and call themselves information architects. But nobody did—until now. Suddenly it's become a ubiquitous term" (Wurman, 2001, p.vi). These movements, one in the direction of self-expression and the other in seemingly the opposite direction, of expressing information clearly, even didactically, are, I believe, both visitations of the same zeitgeist.

The new illustration

Illustration, as design content, is of course not new. The art-poster is widely regarded as the beginning of graphic design as a dedicated practice. The travel posters popular in Europe and Britain in the 1930s are well-known, and illustration, especially line art, has been evident for centuries and was particularly popular with art-directors (and presumably the reading public) throughout the 1940s and 50s, only to be subsumed by photography. What is new in illustration is its remarkable surge back to prominence since 2000. Illustration is in the ascendancy: "The age-old discipline of illustration, or commercial art as some may prefer to call it today, has enjoyed something of a renaissance in recent years. For a discipline that was in a state of crisis and almost on the verge of extinction for the best part of the 1990s, this was a timely resurgence" (Hyland and Bell, 2003, p.7).

What is important for me to demonstrate here is that illustration's reversal of fortune is not as a result of any new-found visual literacy (I will pursue this thread in my Chapter 5) but merely an outcome of the previous decade's experiments. It may seem a long bow to draw to describe deconstructive graphics as the antecedents to the new illustration, after all, their aesthetics are markedly different. The former places the emphasis on typography and its imagery is comprised of photography. The latter, by contrast, places less emphasis on pushing the boundaries of typography (in fact often happily revisits 60s and 70s type, as in Figure 23) and has its non-realistic, illustrated pictorial content to the fore. Further confounding expectations, these recent practitioners resist easy categorization. Rinzen, and Phunk studios, two of the bigger names in early 21st Century illustration graphics, call themselves designers first and foremost. E-boy, widely known for their isometric, pixel-media illustrations don't describe what they do as illustration, rather they say, "We create re-usable pixel objects and take them to build complex and extensible design" ("About", n.d.).

Figure 23: Recent illustrative design, such as this record sleeve by Sanna Annukka, concerns itself with imagery rather than pushing the boundaries of typography

At the same time that deconstructionist graphics were being co-opted into the mainstream 'alternative' music became decidedly mainstream (Markey, 1991). The most conspicuous outlet for youth rebellion that had existed as a concept as long as 'youth' itself, had been effectively removed and placed firmly in the grasp of mainstream marketers and consumers. Where to now for rebellious youth and aspiring rockers? With the title of 'star' conferred upon graphic designers by a media hungry for the next big thing—to help sell newspapers, magazines and advertising space—the visual realm became an avenue through which to aspire: and of course, the new designers were bound to follow on from the 'cool' designers of the 90s. That was, after all, the period in which graphic designers were for the first time lauded as celebrities. If nothing else, the deconstructionist typographers had loosened up the practice of design and allowed it to be a place for play and experimentation rather than formulaic solutions for communication problems. They had pushed design in the direction of art. What do you get when you cross a designer with an artist? Perhaps, an illustrator. Hyland and Bell in *Pen & Mouse*, an early survey of the rising tide of illustration, say that illustration resides in the gap between graphic design and fine art (2001). Illustration certainly gives the designer of a particular inkling more scope to express him or herself than had even the recent movements in typographic design.

In addition to these aspirations of the new designers, the new technologies that arrived in the 80s and 90s allowed new aesthetics which need not necessarily ape their immediate predecessor but may in fact result in much less predictable manifestations: I have mentioned that the logic of the computer might easily have lead to a further consolidation of the grid as the foundation for graphic design. Perhaps it was clear to many new designers that the reinvention of type in the digital medium was an experiment well and truly tested; an idea fully played out. It is certainly difficult to conceive of a typeface that goes beyond the continually randomizing function of Letteror's Beowulf, for example. Such extreme experiments, and the perfect re-mediation of old faces into seamless digital forms seemed to suggest that typography had gone as far as it could and come all the way back again. Perhaps then, only the pictorial elements of graphic communication were ripe for experimentation.

Early on in the growth of new illustration, for the first five years or so of the new millennium, the computer was still the key tool. This seems to be changing as I will discuss below, but for now let us examine the combination of the computer and the illustrator. The introduction of Flash software on top of html coding and web interfaces in the late 1990s resulted in, somewhat perversely, a shift back to a screen-printed aesthetic from the machine age of the 1930s. The new and rapidly spreading web-technologies resulted in a sanguine uptake of the associated aesthetics which place emphasis on flat, outlined shapes within a picture. Flash software on the Internet gives its authors the potential to create full-screen movement with very small file sizes and, accordingly, very short download times for the impatient user viewing the work somewhere else in the world. Here, for the first time is a realisation of photography's liabilities, though only because photography and video of a certain quality and size require large file sizes and long downloads. Flash websites boomed for the first few years of the 2000s:

> the objectivity of the outline style suddenly feels right. You find it in fashion ads in Dazed & Confused magazine and gracing the covers of techno CDs. Arena uses it for tongue-in-cheek illustrated features on executive flying, the future of work and wife swapping in suburbia (interchangeable swingers go through the motions on the stairs, on the kitchen table and even in the loft). Habitat catalogues have offered cute-looking line drawings of the product range for some time. (Poynor, 2001, p.78)

Many of today's young designers are proficient at print design and designing for the Internet. Steve Alexander told me that Rinzen 'cut their teeth' on website design. Flash was the way to make cutting edge sites in the early 2000s. A focus on Flash not only led the team in a particular aesthetic direction, but provided the key portfolio pieces for which future clients chose Rinzen. It makes sense that the aesthetic forms in one space of design are carried over into another, even if they are less appropriate there. The requirement of a small file size for a Flash-based website also leads to decisions about what to leave out. Again, this decision is made for commercial imperatives: the client needs to be sure that their potential audience won't be frustrated, waiting for long periods for a picture to download, and, as ever was the case, the designer needs to take as little time as possible to design and build a quality piece of communication. Poster designers between the wars, in their efforts of making multiple stencils for screen-printing, had to make very similar decisions about what to leave out. It is no coincidence then, that the Flash phenomenon has produced an aesthetic. It is also

THE NEW ILLUSTRATION

no coincidence that this aesthetic resembles closely one we've seen before, though perhaps surprisingly, that aesthetic is from the 1930s (Figure 24 and 25).

Figure 24 and 25: Similarities in the outline style of design for silk-screening (Tom Purvis, 1920s) and recent design informed by Flash. (BJ Ball Art of Contradiction, 2004, illustrator unknown)

In addition, the computer drawing applications—Freehand, Illustrator, Corel Draw—were built with professional illustrators in mind, just as Photoshop was originally tailored to meet the needs of photographers and retouchers. Hence the drawing packages capture the look, to a great degree, of these pre-existing methods of illustration. The work of one of the last ubiquitous, pre-computer illustrators, Patrick Nagel, embodies the cool, 1980s look, (Figure 26). Looking at his work now, and indeed that of another prolific producer of editorial illustration in the early 1980s, Guy Billout, it's hard to imagine that it could have been done without a computer, let alone executed in a pre-computer age. The aesthetic, in other words, takes nothing from computer graphics whatsoever, but instead, completely informs the new computer graphics as they begin to be established. Just as Photoshop was built to emulate the great 'trick photography' techniques that reached their zenith in the Hipgnosis album covers of the 1970s, so Adobe Illustrator was built to capture the stylistics of these superlative illustrators.

Figure 26: Pre-computer graphics: Patrick Nagel's use in the early 1980s of rapidograph pen and flat paint, for consistency of line and colour fill, prefigures the computer graphics tools available in the following decade

In addition, the software enables the accurate tracing of photographs, suggesting a lingering influence of photography as much as an escape from its clutches. This ability to quickly trace source images explains at least some of the new aesthetics: illustrators make pictures with this aesthetic because it is very simple to do so.

More recent trends have seen the adoption of hand-made techniques and a loosening of the grip of the computer for the drawn aspects of the illustration. Vector graphics are no longer the clear leader in this ever-widening field (Klanten & Hellige, 2007, p.184). But the computer is still accessed as a major tool in production and, as were many of the deconstructionist designs of the 90s, many of the current works are visually noisy expressions. As signposts of the zeitgeist they must be telling us something. Perhaps it's as direct a connection as busy illustrations being an appropriate response to a speedy world. Apart from Mareis' acknowledgement that "Illustration's self-perception lies precisely in its difference to photography" (2005, p.4), the illustrators and the editors of recent illustration anthologies seem not to clearly express why these various approaches exist except in the most general, instinctual terms.

The new illustration is the child of deconstruction, in spite of there being little family resemblance. It certainly continues the trend where the client, or at least the client's marketing manager or art director, and not the designer, is making the design decisions through choice of illustrator. And the new illustration is born from a pursuit of design as art, and aesthetic as technological possibility. It has not arrived as a result of research into or discourse about the picture in design. What the new illustrators still lack is a sound theoretical base from which to refute Modernism's prescriptions for pictures.

Information architecture

The polar opposite of the new illustration must be information architecture. The International Institute for Information Design defines information design as the "planning, and shaping of the contents of a message and the environments it is presented in with the intention of achieving particular objectives in relation to the needs of users". Typically, its proponents argue that information be shown effectively rather than merely in an aesthetically pleasant form. The information architects approach is really the credo of the Bauhaus (adopted from the architect, Luis Sullivan): form follows function. While some startling examples, such as the work of John Snow and Charles Joseph Minard, can be found from the nineteenth century, information design, as a systematic approach to visual communication, began in the 1920s when it first found expression through the 'Viennese Method' of Otto Neurath. The work was recommenced most notably in the Tokyo '64 Olympics graphics of Yoshiro Yamashita at the Nippon Design Centre. In the true spirit of information architecture, Yamashita's pictographic approach was undertaken for purely practical reasons to overcome communication difficulties; "because few participants or visitors would be fluent in Japanese" (Fischer & Hiesinger, 1995, p.90). Further celebrated examples of the form come to us through Kinneir & Calvert's U.K. road signage, and through Otl Aicher's work for the Munich Olympics in 1972. More recent works for airports, such as Paul Mijksenaar's designs for Schipol in the Netherlands, and Integral/NORM's Köln-Bonn Airport Identity in Germany, stake a claim for the necessity of information design in the daily lives of modern commuters. Some of these examples will be studied in more depth in the fourth chapter in an effort to explain the communicative effect of extremely distilled pictures. Information design critic and analyst, Edward Tufte's forays into the business world have helped cement a place for information graphics in the working lives of as many as the new illustration seems to be reaching through the glamorous fantasies of fashion magazines.

Figure 27: Nigel Holmes' work exhibits the quintessential indicators of information design: distilled pictures removing visual noise to allow efficient communication

Rather than an extension of the designer-as-artist approach that flowed from the Deconstructionists to the new illustrators, the growth in information design is a reaction against the notion of design as art. It is no coincidence that Richard Saul Wurman witnessed its up-take in the late 1990s just as deconstruction was making in-roads into mainstream graphics. Information design also embodies the zeitgeist of this new machine age: it is a reaction against, among other things, the plethora of 'information' without context. As the Web began to spin its influence across the globe, it was an oft-heard cry that we were gaining data at the expense of knowledge. Richard Saul Wurman himself is known for his *Information Anxiety* (1989) which articulated precisely this fear of unhelpful overload. In 1997, Edward Tufte had suggested that good information design is exactly about turning down the visual noise of this new design age: "Shrill and strident visual activities will tend to dominate the information space, scrambling finely detailed but relevant content" (p.65). He goes on to say that "relevant to nearly every display of data, the smallest effective difference is the Occam's razor ('what can be done with fewer is done in vain with more') of information design" (p.73). Tufte makes a case for the information design approach: "When principles of design replicate principles of thought, the act of arranging information becomes an act of insight" (p.9).

Saul-Wurman and Tufte are the champions of using this approach, not for typography, but importantly for us here, for pictures in the service of information transmission and reception; Saul-Wurman as practitioner, patron and 'art' director, and Tufte as critic. A work executed following this design method is not one the viewer can determine at first glance, through aesthetics alone, to have been generated by an information architect. Rather it is the approach that defines each disparate aesthetic in the field. As Tufte puts it, "Visual representations of evidence should be governed by principles of reasoning about quantitative evidence. For information displays, design reasoning must correspond to scientific reasoning. Clear and precise seeing becomes as one with clear and precise thinking" (p.53). It is not difficult to determine the similarities with the stated aims of the Neue Schweizer Grafik, but also key differences when we look at Müller-Brockmann's credo:

> "The maximum in information will be had if the object or the idea is matter-of-factly and esthetically presented with a minimum of additional forms. Each subjective adornment in the sense of an illustrative exaggeration [should] be avoided, and the graphic form must become, if possible, the anonymous bearer of the message." (Müller, 2000)

Information architects would make no such assumption about minimal information but instead aim for *optimal* information: how much information would make the message easily understood? In some instances, for example, in airport signage where symbols are not fully explanatory but must be learned and culturally agreed upon, a degree of redundancy is required between images and words that actually may work against 'a minimum of forms'.

Information design is the only visual design approach with the stated aim of distillation: that a message should be stripped of any *unnecessary* information which might put its clarity in jeopardy. For this reason I choose to apply the findings of this book to information design in Chapter 4. If one looks at the 100 year history of graphic design, a general trend towards distillation of image is only clearly evident elsewhere in logo design. For example, the original Shell logo appeared as a precise engraving of a pecten shell. Throughout the first half of the 20th Century this sign evolved into the one with which we are familiar. Reasons for this distillation or any other example evident in logo design are nowhere clearly articulated. Either designers did not explain their reasons or design historians, focused, as we have seen, on matters typographic, did not think to record any explanations. Raymond Loewy himself, well-known for his re-designs of the Shell and Lucky Strike identities, could only phrase the concept of distillation in economic terms:

> 'Before—the old Lucky Strike package was dark green. On the obverse was the well-known Lucky Strike red target. The reverse was covered with text that few people read. The green ink was expensive, had a slight smell. After—The new package is white and the red target has remained unchanged. The text on the reverse has been moved to the sides, displaying the red target on both faces. Printing cost has been reduced.' (Hollis, 2001, p.100)

Information design, in contrast to this, seeks to do what—according to the information architects—all graphic design should do: argue for itself beyond merely making a message look good or being driven by commercial considerations, to make the communication work as appropriately as it should in its proposed circumstances. Even here however, in a field of the design discipline where "design reasoning must correspond to scientific reasoning", the role of the picture is never well explained. Also, as I have tried to demonstrate in my next chapter, disagreement is evident between the experts in the field of information design as to how pictures communicate, even in this relatively narrow field of design. This confusion suggests that another way of discussing the role of pictures in design is needed.

Conclusion

Of course, illustration and information are not the only streams of graphic design in operation. A plethora of other approaches exists, including reworked, retro stylings, a range of 'un-designed' vernaculars and even some uneasy Swiss-deconstructionist hybrids (Figure 28). This reworking of styles might be a sign of a new visual freedom through which many positive outcomes might be accidentally achieved through sheer weight of numbers. However, it might just as easily suggest a lack of evolution, a lack of theory or discourse-based exploration to provide a clear direction. One sees, for example, the return even to the Swiss method as a perennial trend. This return, as one of the few obvious directions in contemporary graphics, is evidence of the Swiss having most clearly articulated their approach to design. Any designer adopting the method may argue for it on the grounds that, as Steven Heller echoed in his *Cult of the Ugly* essay, their "method was based strictly on ideas of balance and harmony which hold up under close scrutiny". Proponents of this method state that, like the International Style in architecture, the Swiss method for graphic design survived changes in technology and fashion because of fundamental rules that worked.

CONCLUSION

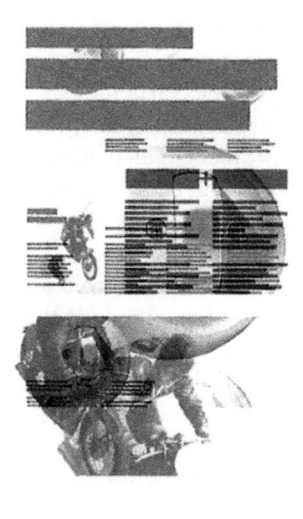

Figure 28: In the work of Müller+Hess, the rich past of 'Neue Schweizer Grafik' ('New Swiss Graphic Design') is available as a tableau of cultural references (from modernist and deconstructionist sources). Here, the motorbikes previously seen in Müller-Brockmann's road safety campaign posters of the 1950s re-emerge with a more illustrative feel derived through tonal drop out and monochrome treatment. Müller+Hess go further to disturb our expectations of the poster form: text becomes picture; graphic content to fill and balance the layout. Readable content is removed to the point of being more opaque even than the most densely overlaid deconstructionist compositions

It seems that the Swiss method abides because it has a clearly articulated position if nothing else. The fact that its position on imagery was less than thoroughly considered does not seem to be of concern to the designers that still use this approach. Perhaps the polish and detail in a sharp photograph merely adds to the slick finish evident in such crisp, clean design. It's apparent then that a reliance on photography that has held sway with designers for at least 70 years is a reliance on the Swiss Method, albeit mediated through various design courses and text books. It seems likely that for contemporary designers, using the decades old techniques of the Swiss, there might also be an element of nostalgia for a time when, at least the forthright visuals suggest, life seemed so much more black and white.

This ability to articulate a position is important to practicing designers, especially when faced with the questioning or criticism of the client who wonders why s/he is paying so much for expertise that can not articulate

77

itself; that can not readily express its own worth. The fact that this expertise is concerned with what is often seen as mere paper or screen-based ephemera only compounds the designer's difficulties.

So, historically and quintessentially, the problem of the designer, in the milieu with the client is a problem of articulation: the designer cannot communicate with the client on a purely visual level. If the client was a competent visual communicator presumably s/he wouldn't need to contract the designer in the first place. The designer that can communicate verbally with the client, speak his or her language, as well as read and write visually, is therefore in a position of strength. The idea that design work is shrouded in magic as some kind of creative act (rather than analytical or based in research and development) or the designer is some kind of mystic given to divine inspiration may seem to have something going for it, but in the end, especially in a business sense, this leads to the kind of argument I put forward earlier: if the client is unhappy s/he can go to another designer: maybe their 'inspired' work will be more suitable: the client then becomes the one making the design decisions. If, however, the designer can communicate by speaking or writing (and not just visually with 'the pitch') as to why a graphic design looks the way it looks, to communicate what it communicates, then it becomes clear to the client what the designer expects to achieve, and clear to the client what s/he is paying for.

A look at precedents and antecedents in this short history has, I hope, shown just how much of graphic design's progress or lack thereof is down to technology. The limitations of technology and attempts to overcome these or to work within them, even revel in them as did the Deconstructionists, and reactions against previous design approaches, have informed graphic design aesthetics in the absence of picture theory. Unless some understanding of pictures is gained (including an understanding that could also extend to type, as we shall see) designers are condemned to reacting against previous movements or reacting to the new technology. Information design is clearly more focused on a didactic outcome for its visual communication. In this sense it has to be clearer about what it does. This articulation of a position is what will ultimately protect it from the vagaries of visual fashion. Wurman's coining of 'Information Architecture' was a deliberate gambit to distance 'serious' design from the shallow surfaces of its commercial mainstream. Illustration, in part marketed on its wistful appeal, seems to be less able to articulate its own strengths. But, if we know more about how pictures work in the first place, and given that information design is often comprised of drawn pictures, perhaps these two streams of contemporary graphic design can be reconciled.

Chapter 4
Information Design
Systems of Seeing

In this chapter I focus on pictures that, on a realism continuum, are furthest removed from photography to see how such pictures can contribute to an understand of visual communication. While I touched briefly on information design in the previous chapter in terms of its relationship to the aesthetics of design history, here I want to look more closely at its communicative potential as a function of distance from realism. As I have explained, a reduction in the kind of detail we associate with the real world and with photography can lead to a different understanding of a visual message. It follows that the pictures furthest removed from photographic realism should be the pictures that most clearly demonstrate such difference. Information designs, which I take to include diagrams and other visual explanations, are generally built from distilled or abstracted pictures such as pictograms and ideograms. These are examined below in terms of what they show us about invisible (and therefore, unphotographable) relationships. In the field of information graphics there is a clear tendency towards the employment of distilled pictures in preference to high-fidelity pictures. Edward Tufte, the foremost analyst and critic of presenting visual explanations, has said this about the elements that make up information design: "By illustrating sequences of action and hidden views, the diagram outperforms eye or camera" (1997, p.57).

INFORMATION DESIGN

In terms of my second chapter, this makes sense. However, it is very difficult to find clear explanation as to why these kinds of pictures are used. Clearly, the popularity of these in this field suggests that the designers of information graphics sense that they have adopted the correct visual mode. But what do the research and the text books say about such pictures in the service of 'visual explanations'? Despite the rhetoric in the field, information design struggles, like all areas of design, to communicate a set of principles about pictures. Even in this field of graphic design which prides itself on pragmatism and didacticism, clear explanation of why some graphics are more appropriate than others is difficult to locate. In some cases there are profoundly different readings of the same graphic.

Figure 29: *Diamonds Were A Girl's Best Friend* infographic by Nigel Holmes, Time Magazine, 1983

For example, Nigel Holmes' graphic at Figure 29 receives applause from his fellow information graphic designer, Duncan Mill, Director of Graphic News, London:

> This two-column graphic sums up the power of infographics. The exhilarating abandon of the floozy Monroe character grabs the reader, then powerful dynamics take over, all within the restrictions of an image surrounded by text, Holmes guides the reader's eye around the data [...] The use of fishnet stockings as the graph background is so clever, not only accurately reflecting the years and dollar values but also echoing the sexy visual joke. The typography is clean and simple, and the use of colour is eye-catching. (Agar, et al, 2003, p.45)

The very same graphic picture, however, attracts the ire of information graphic critic, Edward Tufte:

> chockablock with cliché and stereotype, coarse humour, and a content-empty third dimension. It is the product of a visual sensitivity in which a thigh-graph with a fishnet-stocking grid counts as a Creative Concept. Everything counts but nothing matters. The data-thin (and thus uncontextual) chart mixes up changes in the value of money with changes in diamond prices, a crucial confusion because the graph chronicles a time of high inflation. (1990, p.34)

Where design texts touch specifically on an information graphic's effectiveness in terms of its relationship to realism, it is difficult to find elucidation about this relationship: how it works, and why it works in terms of visual perception and cognition. Rather, these authors seem to struggle to get beyond an inkling that non-realistic pictures can lend something to communication that realism may not; in *Essential Infographics, an Interview with John Grimwade*, (2003) for example:

> I should also emphasise a certain return to the line, to drawing by hand in graphics. I value this a great deal because the absolutely faithful reproduction of reality is not always the best way of presentation. For example, medical illustrations. I prefer a schematic, which is much easier to understand than those hyper-realistic presentations where the body seems to have been cut in half and photographed. For me, the schematic gives a hierarchy to the information and invites me to enter further into the graphic. This is the language of infographics, which is not the same as photography. (Errea, p.17)

Grimwade's suggestion of some kind of meaningful difference between the picture language of information graphics and the picture language of photographs is left as a tantalising clue, but apart from the mention of hierarchy, no deep exploration is given in that text. And in another instance, a design theorist ponders the amount of realistic detail in a picture, described as the picture's 'information level': "The graphic means used to present an image and its information level become important components of the communication" (Meggs, 1992, p.19). Edward Tufte, says: "Multiple layered views exemplify the special power of diagrams, a capacity to show places or activities that we are unable to see directly from one fixed viewpoint in the real world" (1997, p.57). This suggests that a reduction in realism in no way compromises the communicative potential of the image experience, quite the opposite.

A look at those designers who have made their names or careers developing information design programs based upon this distillation process gives us some further evidence that the instinct to distil is well-founded. Concrete reasons, however, remain difficult to unearth. Otto Neurath, whose famous Isotype work (designed by Gerd Arntz) at least appears to have a coolly scientific basis, had this to say about how we 'read' pictograms: "The first glance: The most important qualities of an object are perceived. The second glance: The less important qualities of an object are perceived. The third glance: additional details are perceived" (cited in Abdullah & Hübner, 2006, p.20). This suggests some understanding of the human visual system: that it is uninterested in high levels of detail, at least initially, but no further explanation is given, other than, "A silhouette compels us to look at essential details and sharp lines; there are no indefinite backgrounds or superfluities" (Neurath, 1946, p.96). The basis for creating his Isotype figures however, rather than being scientific, seems to have been with Neurath since his childhood; he was especially fond of Egyptian hieroglyphics (Pendle, "Otto Neurath's Universal Silhouettes", n.d.). Indeed, rather than specifically following a perceptual theory from the beginning, Neurath suggests that he and his team arrived at the notion of abstractions incrementally:

> At first our symbols were drawn realistically, but by using a new technique we soon simplified them without losing their self-explanatory qualities. We began to cut out our symbols—silhouettes of animals and ploughs and men—from coloured paper, necessarily reducing the outlines to a minimum and avoiding internal lines wherever possible. (1946, pp.97-98)

And here at least some of the motivation for reduction of detail is purely mechanical; to avoid difficulties while manually creating small graphics.

While Neurath tested his visual experiments, and, he makes clear, "Some of our observations were made by students of psychology" (1946, p.99), these observations were made after the graphics had been designed and were on display. The process of design was a process of 'trial and error', according to Paul Rotha, one of Neurath's long-term collaborators. Neurath's overriding consideration, and that of his followers, Modley in the United States and Bliss in Australia, was to create a visual code that could transcend language barriers. Lamenting the demise of hieroglyphics, Neurath said: "I was sorry that the old picture writing had gradually fallen into disuse instead of becoming the basis of an international picture language. The problem of an international language attracted me fairly early" (p.96). Neurath predicted a future where communicating with pictograms would become a necessity. The key to making such a language using symbols other than letters seemed to lie in abstract symbols rather than realistic pictures: "I liked being able to combine similar symbols in different ways without destroying their visual power. This active element belongs also in a special sense to writing when it is regarded as the putting together of single words" (p.97).

The quest for an international visual 'Esperanto' was continued in the design of the pictograms for the 18th Olympic Games, in Tokyo, 1964 (designed in 1962 by Yoshiro Yamashita). As host for the first Olympic Games held in Asia, the Japanese organized a committee headed by the design critic Masaru Katsumi to coordinate the graphic program. Because few participants or visitors would be fluent in Japanese, a program of pictograms was devised to designate the events and services, and it was essential that its visual vocabulary be easily comprehensible. (Fischer & Hiesinger, 1994, p.90)

However, it is difficult in the literature to find coherence in the approaches to this quest for universal picture languages. Those designers well-known for exploring the possibilities do not present a united front. According to his biographer (Rathgeb, 2006, p.114), Otl Aicher, designer and coordinator of the graphics program for the 1972 Olympics in Munich, developed his pictograms based on his readings of Charles Morris's *Theory of*

Signs and on the research of Martin Krampen, a German communications scientist (p.118). Aicher also appears to have liaised with Katsumi, the co-ordinator of the Tokyo '64 graphics program (p.136). While Neurath had suggested minimal abstraction of images for the creation of pictograms, believing this would allow understanding without an accompanying learning curve, Maldonado (a colleague of Aicher's at the Ulm HfG) supported greater abstraction for the creation of pictograms in order to avoid confusion. Maldonado had also assumed a learning process would be inevitable for the reader to familiarise themselves with any pictograms (p.118). According to Rathgeb, however:

> Aicher's pictograms lie somewhere between these two positions. In addition to graphic reduction and a systematization of form, Aicher achieved a high level of variability within the same system by connecting the formal vocabulary with a system of syntax. A central tool of Aicher's methodical approach, in particular for his set of symbols, was a design grid. (p.118)

More on Aicher's grid system later in this Chapter, for now I want only to say that in all of this, the designers of these distilled forms, and their biographers, seem to understand that these forms communicate differently from realistic pictures, but not precisely why. Aicher's research appears to have been very methodical, but a scientific or interpretive basis for the difference between realism and abstraction is not documented other than through a mention of "field research on visual perception of symbols by individuals of different cultural backgrounds". The focus of this simplification was again to create an internationally understandable language rather than to exploit particular known visual faculties; as Rathgeb states, "Aicher tried to prevent his signs from being linked with the cultural context of the original image, which would make it valid only temporarily or in certain cultures" (p.118).

As recently as 2006, *Pictograms, Icons & Signs*, focusing on these distilled pictures, makes a synthesis of Neurath and Aicher to propose a picture language "in the context of globalisation" (Abdullah, R. and Hübner, R., 2006, p.228). Three quarters of a century on from Neurath and Arntz, the authors' motivation, rather than one based on recent discoveries about the human visual system, seems precisely the same: "pictograms will inevitably become a more common area of design" (p.7). Many impressive contemporary and historical examples are shown, some of which are examined in detail later in this book, but the authors are content to explain how to design pictograms without reference to the question of how we are able to perceive these pictures. The book culminates in a lesson on using icon language by Professor Jochen Gros (another alumni of Ulm) to devise a global, visual language, to realise Neurath's aim (p.228).

Jock Kinneir and Margaret Calvert's well-known road sign system for the United Kingdom, in contrast, seems to have been aimed more at the parochial audience:

> Many of [Calvert's] illustrations were inspired by aspects of her own life. The cow featured in the triangular sign warning drivers to watch out for farm animals on the road was based on Patience, a cow on her relatives' Warwickshire

83

farm. Eager to make the school children crossing sign more accessible, she replaced the image of a boy in a school cap leading a little girl, with one of a girl – modelled on a photograph of herself as a child – with a younger boy. Calvert described the old sign as being: "quite archaic, almost like an illustration from Enid Blyton ... I wanted to make it more inclusive because comprehensives [English co-educational schools] were starting up." ("Jock Kinneir + Margaret Calvert", n.d.)

In terms of their interest in the simplicity of pictures, Calvert and Kinneir were concerned with legibility at speed and, apparently economic concerns were still an issue. "Style never came into it. You were driving towards the absolute essence. How could we reduce the appearance to make the maximum sense and minimum cost?" With regard to the 'internationality' of these abstracted pictures, Neurath came closest to explaining their utility over more realistic pictures. For Neurath, like the advocates of Die Neue Schweizer Grafik, the photograph was neutral but unlike the Swiss School, Neurath found the photograph unhelpful since it treated its contained information un-hierarchically. The Isotype figures on the other hand were designed to allow a systematic and repeatable method of building visual meanings without the diverting detail that photography tends to capture (Neurath, 1973).

Why simplified pictures work in complex communication

Connie Malamed's *Visual Language for Designers* succinctly explains how one puts to work much of the theory. For example, she directs the designer to, in turn, "direct the eyes" of the reader of information design through careful placement of the elements. She tells designers to "organise for perception" their graphic compositions; and, importantly, she instructs designers to "reduce realism" in their work in order to turn down visual noise. What I seek to do here is further explain, not the how, but the why. In my second chapter I referred to some of the psychological faculties that allow the understanding of abstracted or distilled pictures. The reasons given there, combined with our conceptual model, the realism continuum, can help us to better understand why the typical approaches taken in information design can be effective, especially in explaining relationships between things.

As the visual communicator considers pictures removed from realism, several communicative opportunities present themselves. The designer can begin to impose some order upon the pictures s/he creates. The degree to which the designer departs from realism is directly proportional to how much imposition of order is afforded. What exactly does visual 'ordering' entail? According to Albarn and Miall Smith in *Diagram: The Instrument of thought,* ordering is understanding: "Without doctrinaire connotations, it implies qualitative judgements based on harmony of function as observed in the whole pattern [...] its success or 'realness' is measured by its usefulness" (1977, pp.7-8). On the realism continuum, diagrams, or information designs as these are called here, sit at the opposite end from photographic realism. The most realistic picture (removed from the object itself) is the colour photograph of whatever the object happens to be. At the other end of the scale is the arbitrary graphic (Wileman, 1993; Gropper, 1963; Knowlton, 1966) or the icon (McCloud). It is these distilled pictures that are the modules upon which diagrams or information designs are built. Information designs are the visual result of travelling along this continuum, removing detail in the process. This stripping away of realistic detail is best described as distillation rather than simplification, since it is not a process of removing information across the entire image so much as taking away unnecessary detail so the designer and the reader can focus on and put into some order the attributes of the picture pertinent to the intended communication. This allows the resulting picture to amplify particular meanings in a way that realistic pictures can not. For example, an increase in line weight for outlines and a reduction in the number of shapes and colours can be used to amplify connections that are less apparent in the real world.

Information designs, the kinds of visual material at the end of this process of abstraction and distillation, allow a deeper intellectual connection with visual material than is prompted by realism. At the very least, a reduction in realism must prompt a search for meaning beyond the representational. This could be described as *seeing with the mind* as opposed to merely seeing with the eyes.

Dichotomy between realism and diagram

An analysis of the visual modes of photography and information design as opposites on this realism continuum reveals that these continue to compete on a range of levels, and that photography's real strengths are limited to fewer applications than its *lingua franca* status would suggest. Photographs are particularly good at environmental portraiture (Heller and Pomeroy, 1997, p.46) and communicating aspects of travel, and sensual subjects such as foods and textures because these things require photography's ability to stencil a trace of the real thing (Sontag, 1977, p.154). A visceral appearance generated through photographic recording not only transmits specific visual experience effectively, it also enables cross-sensual appreciation of the scene: photography is very good at capturing specifics of atmosphere. For example, recording the condensation on a glass of white wine, can stimulate, through sight, the other senses of touch and taste. However, through an examination of the following dichotomies: Decontextual/Contextual; Specific/General; Secretive/Revelatory, we see that the reduction in realism required to move from one end of the realism continuum to the other allows for more precise communication, paradoxically, through being less faithful to reality.

Decontextual/contextual

A good diagram should have some rules or a strategy imposed upon it according to Tufte (1990, p.37). This is the essence of 'ordering' as described above. Peter Grundy, information designer for the Guardian UK newspaper, told me that he sees this kind of ordering as a manipulation of drawn imagery until complex things can be made simple to see and understand. To make order out of the content, some visual rules need to be adopted or invented by the information designer. These rules can result in a range of visual forms, but each could be described as a 'system of drawing' (Hardie, 2005, pp.126-138) which we could easily describe as a 'system of seeing' that the designer applies to the content, to impose visual cohesion on the disparate elements requiring depiction. I mentioned in the introduction to this book that pictures seem to be far more elusive than type in regard to laying down laws to obey or to break. Some of the more effective examples of information design exhibit visual rules which their designers invent and then exploit to great, cohesive effect. Some visual examples will help to illustrate this point.

From gestaltist experiments we know that the mind relates objects of a similar shape and orientation (Figure 30). Similarly, an isometric rule used in the information design at Figure 31 allows all the machines to appear as if they have some relationship. In the real world, these machines may share a space and similar colours, they may not, but they are likely to be somewhat different shapes and certainly could not all be viewed at once at the same angle. The reduction in realism that enables these disparate objects to be rendered in the same manner allows us to conceive of them as part of a system (the connections between the machines is also made clear through the use of the abstract symbols, dotted lines and arrows) and that the system works and works efficiently.

Figure 30: In addition to the mind relating shapes of similar colour and shape, it recognises a hierarchy in these gestalt patterns of belonging: colour trumps shape. In the set at left, similar shapes belong together. In the set at right, colour overrides shape to suggest that the red objects are now a set, the blue another, etc

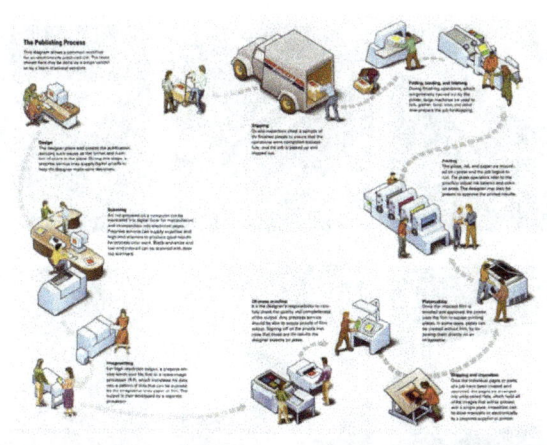

Figure 31: Steve McGuire, illustration for The Publishing Process in Working With Prepress and Printing Suppliers (AGFA Digital Color Prepress volume three, 1993, pp.2-3)

Otl Aicher's pictogram designs for the Munich Olympics were built upon a strict, regular grid that allowed only a limited use of angles and curves. From this basis a small number of modular parts were derived that could be reassembled to make up the different sporting events of the games. In this way order was imposed upon the visual representation of the disparate activities that happen at the Olympics.

In the Bell Telephone Book illustrations at Figure 32, the graphics function through a less radical reduction in realistic detail. The ordering is not so severe. This time a tone drop-out or 'threshold' approach is used rather than a forced reshaping of the objects. This can still be described as a system of seeing: Objects are viewed from a consistent angle; light is supplied from a consistently positioned source, and; each object is posed in a manner intended to reveal the most relevant information about that object. Again, it is the reduction in realism that makes each of these objects, visually disparate in reality, appear as if they belong to a larger set because this reduction allows for amplification of gestalt qualities of colour (here, strictly black and white), shape, line and orientation to come to the fore. In other words, it is precisely the reduction in realism that allows for the imposition of a system of seeing, and such a system in turn allows a sense of belonging that would not be so readily apparent in the real world. In the case of the telephone book graphics, this particular, subtle ordering allows the introduction of an infinite range of new objects to be added to the catalogue. Illustrators following the system of seeing laid down by the designers need simply model the object in three-quarter view and render it in black and white.

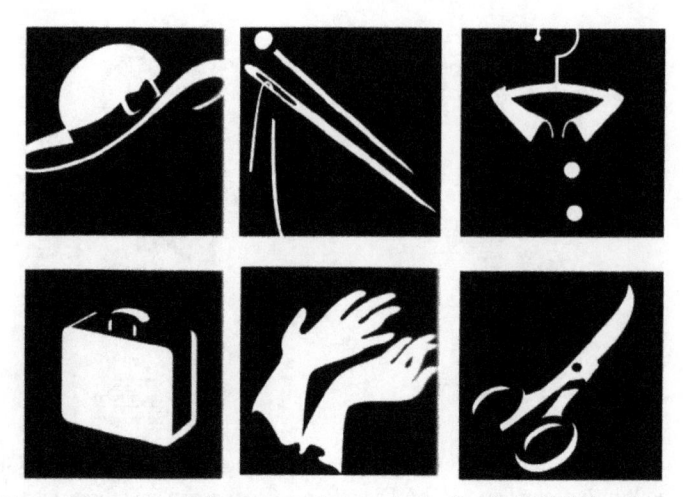

Figure 32: Joachim Müller-Lancé, pictographs for Pacific Bell Yellow Pages. (Abdullah and Hubner, 2006, p.144)

The reduction in realism provides for the contextualisation for objects when we, as visual communicators, decide which belongs with which. In the real visual world, these connections would not be so apparent. Realistic visual means, such as photography, tend to merely reflect this apparent disconnectedness (Figure 33).

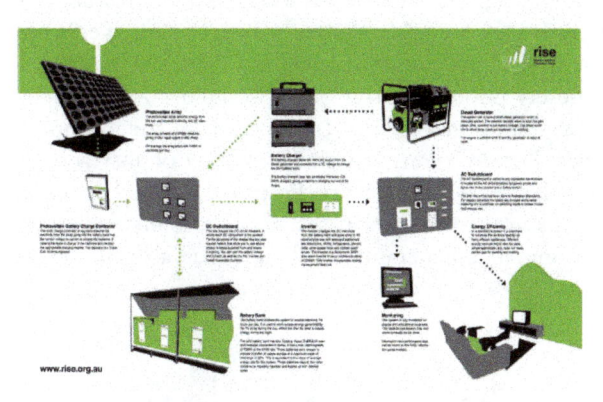

Figure 33: Photographic content for systems visualisation (above) is incapable of suggesting the connectedness that a drawing lends via a limited palette and a consistent drawing style (below). Furthermore, the drawing can be used to capture only the salient parts of the system while photography tends to capture visual noise specific to the background of each subject

Specific/general

Another problem with photography is the specificity of its output. From its 19th century infancy, photography's role was hotly debated. One of the important strands of argument was concerned with photography's specificity, and the application of soft-focus techniques to make it less so (Green-Lewis, 1996, p.55). The quarrel was particularly heated between those who argued that photography could take the place of Pre-Raphaelite painting's inventive story-telling (p.4), and those who maintained that photography's logical role was documentary: That it should be used to capture the world as it existed since photography allowed that, at last, a shared vision of the world could be had (p.26), and that photography could record the world, unmediated by the human hand, through "optical and chemical means alone" (p.59). The design community has continued using photography for story-telling, especially in the advertising arena, regardless of the reasonably well-documented arguments put by the early documentary advocates. Stock photography rates a special mention here since we are concerned with photography, not as art, but as a tool for the communication designer. The application of stock photography in design illuminates this problem. The business of stock photography is predicated on the notion that a single photograph has the potential for multiple applications (Lupton & Miller, 1999):

> A happy family holding hands and gazing at their new home may have been shot to sell real estate, but when [the photograph] is offered for use in a catalogue it may be used for its symbolic dimension rather than its literal content. The same photo could be used to sell life insurance, government bonds, or aluminium siding. (p.128)

As Lupton and Miller observe however, in stock photography, the information contained in a picture is at odds with this drive towards generic applications (p.133). It is no coincidence that we see the use of editorial illustration and diagram in situations where concepts are difficult to grasp through photography (merely 'pointing at things') or would become too specific if shown through representational means. In contrast, in the example at Figure 34, The designer, Peter Grundy has chosen a level of abstraction which disallows our impulse to try and identify these characters. The features are so abstracted we instantly give up that task and focus instead on what the characters are doing. The generality implied by the abstraction makes us look instead at the actions performed in each cartoon.

Figure 34: Peter Grundy. Set of icons for the Princess Alexander Hospital website accentuating action over specific identity

Secretive/revelatory

Wileman proposed that there were at least three ways of depicting objects; through pictorial, graphic and verbal symbols. But 'objects' are not the only things that can be depicted. What happens when we want to make pictures of things that don't have an image in the real, visible world? Things that are conceptual rather than concrete? Where there is nothing to gesture towards by way of an explanation, that is, there is nothing in the real world that can be seen and therefore photographed, it does not follow that there is nothing there to be visually communicated. For example, it may be impossible to point at something in a modern office space and pronounce that a particular worker or strata of the organization is clearly subordinate to another. However, through the less realistic visual modes of illustration or diagram we have the means to express visually that which cannot be readily photographed but is understood by the employees and pictured in their minds' eye. A corporate structure diagram easily makes visible the well-known but visually indistinct differences between workplace strata, in the same way that a family tree, another common information design, expresses the relationship of individuals to a larger organization. This is, in essence, an extreme example of Gombrich's pictures that 'function in the narrative' rather than accurately match any real world referent. In this case, there is no visible referent to match.

Photographs may have gained an "insuperable power to determine what people recall of events" (Sontag, 2004) and yet, photographs can not possibly capture whole relations or economies within the social realm because such interactions are often invisible. Anthony Woodiwiss (2001), makes a sharp distinction between vision and visuality. Vision, in essence, is that which we see in the world around us which purports to be unmediated; a view of the world which could be described as empirical or observable, even photographable. Visuality on the other hand is a way of describing the world through structural models which help us to understand its workings. This difference, between what we see with our eyes, and what we can make visual in our minds, has a political dimension. In an obvious example, we are reminded of Marx's "famous architectural metaphor of base and superstructure" (p.38), which is essentially a relational diagram. Hazel Henderson's Layer Cake with Icing is a political model that works in a similar way because it makes visual that which is not photographable or able to be represented in a realistic manner. Henderson explains that:

> The icing on the top is the private sector, which rests on the layer below, the public sector. The top two layers are the only ones economists typically measure. But in this analysis, there are two lower layers that are non-monetized and invisible to economists, but which are really supporting the whole thing. These include the Love Economy (unpaid productive work like raising children and maintaining the household, serving on the school board, do-it-yourself housing, rehab) and Mother Nature, the vast wealth of biodiversity that keeps our air and water clean and provides all the food and bread and resources we need to sustain life, which go completely uncounted. (Mau, 2004, pp.135-136)

One can not go out and photograph either Marx's or Henderson's model, but through a diagrammatic explanation these visual metaphors may be fixed upon the page or screen.

A little developed mode of visual communication is a hybrid of cartoon styles put to use to describe complex relationships or systems where diagrams borrow from illustrative styles, for example, employ some conventions of comics (Figure 35). There is an inherent honesty in non-realistic visual modes proportional to their distance from realism: Immediately upon seeing a picture that is clearly not photographic, the reader knows it was authored by someone. There is no denial of authorial voice, and so, such a picture may be critiqued as being only one person's point-of-view. On the one hand information design has been set up by its godfather (Richard Saul Wurman) at a deliberate distance from graphic design and illustration: its arty, aesthetically conscious cousins, and has tended to have an aseptic appearance not far removed from the bar graphs and pie charts at its base. However, if the stated aim of much of this field is to communicate, or in the terms of Hans Rosling, a professor of global health, to 'liberate the data' trapped in dense and unfathomable tabular and statistical formats, maybe illustration can help accelerate this accessibility. Information designs or diagrams that have a clearly drawn nature, rather than being constructed from the ready-made geometric primitives available in Microsoft Office or even more sophisticated drawing software, clearly declare and reveal their conceptual and constructed nature.

All pictures are subjective, are the work of someone (Wurman, 2001, p.31), so it follows that the pictures to be trusted are the ones that explain by their very appearance that they have been 'made up'. On the other hand, since its early history, accounts of photography tended to separate the photographer from the photograph and empower the photograph as an independent print of the world. Photography can distort a message through pretending that it's not structured, by pretending there is no author's voice or agenda. When the visual communicator is confined to using realistic pictures only, he or she is effectively attempting to communicate by pointing at objects. This is essentially what realism allows. To explain the shortcomings of such a means of visual communication, Goldsmith (1984, p135) tells of her analysis of Schonell's (1932) *Essential Spelling List*. His list comprises around 400 words which he proposed form the basic vocabulary for children. Goldsmith says, "I could find only about 120 words that could be directly illustrated (of which only eighty could be called reliable)". Even at an early age then, children's language is already dealing with non-object words. In other words, realistic pictures, at best, will easily illustrate only about one third of the written language for children. As we grow and learn more of the world and our vocabulary develops, an even smaller percentage of words are used to deal with concrete things: As children we have encountered many of these objects, but we have not encountered many of the subtleties of, for example, social interaction. We must be able to picture verbs as well as nouns.

Making the claim for interpretation over perception, Lupton and Miller tell us, "perception is filtered by culture" (1999, p.63). This might suggest that the interpretive view leads to a better understanding of graphic design as a social activity. However, their observation should by no means exclude the use of perceptual psychology in the reading of these kind of graphics, nor should it preclude the social application of graphics built using a method based in perceptual psychology. I have aimed to demonstrate here that a perceptual view of design can also lead to a better understanding of how pictures and diagrams can communicate in the social sphere. Where illustration and information design can be reconciled, at this diagrammatic level, real potential exists for the use of low-fidelity, non-realistic pictures.

Wicked Problems

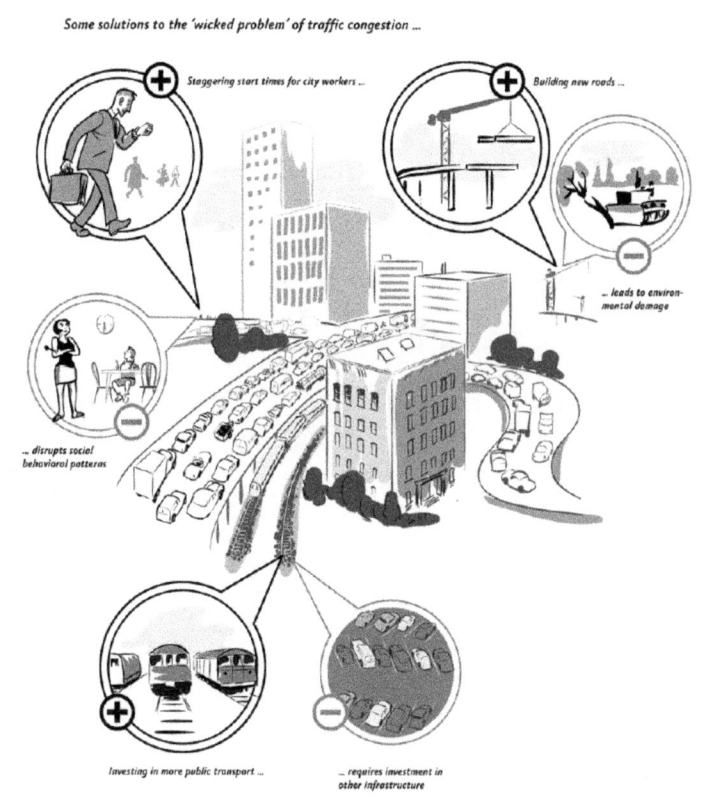

Figure 35: Medley. Illustrations for Christopher Crouch and Jane Pearce's book, *Doing Research in Design*. The pictures eschew the diagrammatic clichés so often employed in visual research rhetoric, in favour of approachable imagery that reminds the reader that design is always about people

Chapter 5
Visual Literacy and Pictorial Strategies

I have explained in my Chapter 3 that illustration is experiencing new-found popularity at the time of writing. However, rather than this indicating a new visual literacy abroad in the field of communication design, I argued that the rise in popularity of illustration was a progression from the designer-as-artist phenomenon of the 1990s. I will focus on this aspect of contemporary commercial visuality in order to make clear that quantity and ubiquity alone are not necessarily evidence of a long-deserved appreciation by editors and clients of illustration's communicative potential. As I focused on the unique ways in which information design can communicate in the previous chapter, here I will focus on illustration as the other clear manifestation of post-modern pictorial design. Unlike information design however, the role of illustration in the communication economy is much less clear. In fact plenty of the new illustration short-circuits the old relationships between illustrator, art director and client, and is pressed into service, like pop music, to promote only itself and its maker. In this regard it is not an element of graphic design as we have known it but more of a convergence of urban art, character design and old-fashioned doodling. In other words not all illustration today is necessarily 'illustrating' anything in the sense of the definition in the introduction to this book.

Visual literacy and the new illustration

Where illustration still sits within the traditional relationship between artist, art director and client, its popularity is also experiencing re-growth, tellingly, in the leading fashion magazines (Klanten & Hellige, 2005) where its presence indicates its modish popularity but not necessarily much else. As Ruddigkeit (2003) observes, "The stream of pictures from photographical archives seems to have been replaced by a revival of illustration. We have rediscovered the power of the individual and personal appeal of illustration in advertising and graphic design". Given this book's undercurrent of prescribing illustration for more design tasks than those for which it is currently deployed, the author should be delighted with this new concentration of and on illustration. However, the terms in which illustration is couched here are rather telling. As with the many comments about drawing, illustration and diagram I have shown previously, applied throughout the history of design criticism, the above remark serves to accentuate that illustration's appeal lies in the mysterious and the subjective. These terms are not helpful to stress the special communicative potential of drawings, nor do illustrators help themselves when they play along. It is not enough to be surrounded by illustration and to be using it for more design tasks; designers and art directors need to know why they are using it if they are to be confident it is communicating what they think it is communicating. Should illustration again fall out of fashion (as it did during the rise of the Neue Schweizer Grafik), it will be difficult to argue for its reinstatement unless its strengths are known and its use can be endorsed on the basis of those strengths. How might these strengths be identified? In the context of creating strategies to improve visual literacy among students, the visual literacy theorists exhort the showing of examples, but at the same time we should be clear on what the examples are showing. As Ausburn and Ausburn explain, to be visually literate is to be able to tell the difference between the "superficial and the valuable messages" (1994, p.288). This distinction may seem unfairly judgmental. Let me try to be clearer and more constructive about the difference. Crouch (2008) sees visual literacy as an active process which may be "developed so that it involves a critically analytical reading of visual texts" (p.195). In the field of graphic design I think there is licence to add "and the *creation* of visual texts", while being mindful of the linguistic bias of the word 'text' in this visual field. Firstly in this chapter I will look at some of the illustrations thrown up by the new-found popularity of the drawn pictures. If these contemporary illustrations can be analysed using the parameters of this book, then those parameters can be added to strategies to improve visual literacy. In light of what I have shown in the previous chapters, I will attempt to refine and augment the work of the visual literacy lobby specifically as it obtains to realism. Rather than take all illustration as evidence that its makers are visually literate, I will, later in this chapter, choose examples which illuminate particular faculties of the human visual system, since this has been the principle focus of this book. This aspect of what it means to be visually literate has previously been overlooked. I will, in the last part of this chapter, study some exemplars of high visual literacy according to values built upon my research. I will analyse a handful of single picture visual texts and some comic strips which I intend will each show something meaningful about a picture's distance from realism.

Firstly, illustrations from the recent crop of celebrated artists are examined to establish what makes these different to the illustrations that come from the previous century. I must state that it is very difficult to talk about the vast range of contemporary, commercial picture-making using any catch-all descriptions. Not only is there a wide variety of aesthetics that have been pursued over the last decade, but the motivations for this kind of work vary greatly, even among the few practitioners that I have interviewed. It would be tempting, and perhaps not incorrect to label these new works as art, rather than illustration. 'Illustration' implies something is being illustrated and this is not always the case here. However, many of the artists practicing this approach—where illustrations essentially promote the artist rather than a client's message— also find themselves working for major, global clients. Deanne Cheuk, for example, has generated her own artworks and publications, but has also been commissioned to art direct magazines and to create murals for major shopping precincts in Japan and the US. Rinzen work in a similar way, creating their own works but then working in that same style to create environments for hotel interiors. Many of the contemporary illustrators' works are connected to graphic design (as it may have once been) through an aesthetic rather than through the artist's *modus operandi*. These are artists who wield design tropes, repurposing the familiar visuals of popular culture and commercial art to create new meanings. Patrick Thomas honed his style through illustrating news articles. Appropriating existing, iconic pictures was one way to meet short deadlines on a weekly basis. He explained to me that one of his ideas was to avoid adding to the world of pictures because there are already enough 'out there' through which a designer can express his opinions. In addition, the use of existing pictures allows the thoughtful designer to trigger associative responses in his audience, whereby, "you can meet them halfway because you know what they know about [the picture]". In the print at Figure 36, Thomas uses a part to stand for a whole: a guitar refers to the realm of rock'n'roll, and a Kalashnikov rifle stands for violent resistance. Overlaying the two invites comparison; perhaps, between ways of changing the world, between means to revolution. Thomas is adept at visual rhetoric, what Gui Bonsiepe describes in his list of *visual verbal figures* as *synecdoche* and *visual verbal comparison*. In other, perhaps less visually literate hands though, the entirety of the post-postmodern visual world, and even those few articles of visual expression that might be thought to provide particular affects in their audiences—dark colours for sombre themes, smooth shapes for calming effects, and so on—are now grist to the mill of the modern illustrator.

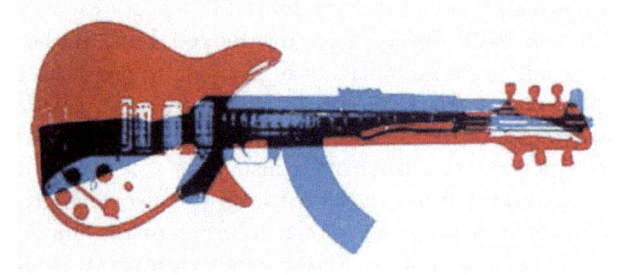

Figure 36: John Lennon's Rickenbacker overlays an AK-47 in a knowing use of pre-existing pictures composed by Patrick Thomas

Picture-making without a brief

The problems of definition that any theory must grapple with are compounded here because the correct labels don't yet exist for this new way of making pictures, nor for the pictures so created. *Pop Art* seems like a sensible label since the motivations behind these recent works might be similar. However, that label refers strongly to a particular historical art movement rather than to a contemporary zeitgeist. Perhaps the Swiss canon regarding graphic design is so long ago refuted that a general free-for-all is permitted. Arisman (2004) says that today's illustrators "have been trained to see, trained to tell stories in time, trained in the craft of picture making, but don't know what to do with this ability outside of the frame of assigned work. We have come face-to-face with the demon of self-content" (p.13).

As I tried to show in my Chapter 3, the recent boom in illustration had a direct antecedent in the designer-as-artist phenomenon of the 1990s. To criticise these illustrators as not playing ball—for not making designs for clients or for stepping outside, from time to time, the accepted economies of the design practice—will not cause them to cease and desist. This is, after all, the creative work of human beings experimenting with ways of seeing, a natural and recurring urge of the artistic throughout history. Instead it's better to see where these drawings can take visual communication and what they might reveal on the way about themselves or about pictures which do attempt to impart particular messages. The new illustrators, like any artist, as Gombrich tells us, are testing the schema; creating their own vocabulary of forms that function in their own narratives. In some ways the new illustration is further removed from visualising a particular message than was the design of the Deconstructionists. Much of the new work is an end in itself rather than pictures which illustrate particular pieces of text in designs or written articles. In this sense, such work is redolent of pop music: a promotional form which might entertain but exists to advertise itself as a throw-away commodity (Clarke, 1995). As I shall demonstrate, this is a particularly pertinent analogy with several of the recent illustrative works.

The designer-as-artist phenomenon has spawned a weird hybrid. Typical aesthetics may involve multiple small elements—often sampled and 're-mixed' from other sources—and abundant colours combined together into a larger and more chaotic scene. Clarity is not a requirement since these graphics often carry no message at all other than one of self-reference (Figure 37). This self-promotional trend is perpetuated by design trade journals such as IdN, and several popular websites, including Canada's Drawn.ca (that it was voted Best Canadian Weblog of 2007 confirms the new-found popularity of illustration) which are devoted solely to illustration, but focus on the creators rather than the editorial or other contexts for which the pictures may have been created.

Figure 37: Aqui Uzumaki self-promotional flyer by Friends With You

This over-abundance of imagery in the service of self-perpetuation is celebrated in several quarters. *Maximalism*, is a book produced by design publisher Rotovision dedicated to this phenomenon and its visual content reveals a bridge between deconstructionist design and the new illustration: "Maximalism celebrates richness and excess in graphic design following years of minimalist rule. A profusion of color and luxury brimming with excess is demanding a return to sensuality [...] for decoration, luxury and fantasy" (Rivers, 2004).

The desire to break free of past constraints is mirrored in the recent explosion of collectible figures (Figure 38) decorated by designers seeking to escape two-dimensionality. A quick survey of the recent styles of illustration and the styles of 3D design for these toys shows a strong visual correlation. The toys too are visual promotions for themselves—they more often than not have no back-story provided by a comic or animated film—and are left to drift between contexts. Jody Boehnert (2006) examines collectible character design as a parallel phenomenon to 'remixed' graphics. Many young graphic designers are involved in the creation of both:

> A beginners' guide to this sometimes bewildering graphic universe might feature Hello Kitty, Rob Reger's Emily the Strange and James Jarvis's In-Crowd. Contemporary character design, abstracted and reduced to the essentials, samples and remixes existing visual codes. Disney characters are not welcome here; nor are the alternative comics characters of the past century, such as Fritz the Cat or Tank Girl. Pictoplasma is defining the perimeters of a new genre. Jamie Hewlett [Tank Girl designer] may make the Design Museum's criteria (as winner of the 'Designer of the Year Prize') but his characters do not appear in the Pictoplasma archive. Lars Denicke of Pictoplasma explains: 'We are looking for iconic characters that gain their meaning through their design, its reduction and anthropomorphic appeal and through their setting, and not so much through a genre and its narrative implications. (Boehnert, "Emotion Graphics", 2006)

Figure 38: Ghostboy, custom paper toy, by Eeshaun in collaboration with Sharim Gubbles from Crossville

Boehnert speaks of sampling and remixing, formerly terms associated with pop music. Rinzen, a design studio from Brisbane, now based in Berlin, believes that design and illustration are, like pop music, 'up for grabs' and can be 'remixed' (Figure 39). Rinzen seems well aware that illustration can be the new rock 'n' roll as its exhibition projects take their names from well-known pop singles such as the Monkees/Neil Diamond's, Daydream Believer. The collective has embarked on several projects where illustrations have been put forward by one design studio to be worked over by another. According to Rilla and Steve Alexander, The RMX project was born from a need to experiment with vision (and sound) outside of the constraints of their daily lives as nascent corporate identity designers (albeit with some time spent at Inkahoots, the famous Brisbane-based, not-for-profit, socially focused design studio). According to Rinzen's own press, "RMX breathes life into the exquisite corpse. 39 international players render a surrealist panorama, a 3.6metre long, 120mm high frieze available as a 5-part poster pack. Shrinkwrapped 360mm x 120mm package." (FreshRMX, n.d.)

Figure 39: Rinzen's Fresh RMX project

The mention of the corpse, apart from being a reference to the surrealists, suggests a kind of cool detachment, even nihilism. This attitude is in keeping with one of the common themes of the new illustration and the associated collectibles: The mutilation of cuteness. This is a kind of hyper-punk sensibility that sees vandalism done to the images of childhood (Figures 40 and 41). Since alternative rock music went mainstream in the early 90s, there has been less viable musical space in which youth can rebel. The visual avenue is one in which frustrations can be vented and a virtual vandalism or violence can be indulged.

Far from the visually literate graphic grit that accompanied the punk movement of the 70s and the later grunge phenomenon of the early 90s, this kind of illustration and design often features all the colours of the rainbow expressed through friendly, curving lines and rounded shapes. Sinister content is couched in upbeat and decorative visual excess. If synaesthesia occurs in all of us as Ramachandran proposes, then these designs are contradicting themselves, perhaps deliberately but perhaps unknowingly. Their lack of explication prevents either assessment. Rinzen, for example says of each of its RMX projects, only that it "follows its own rules" (Showroom: Character Design, 2004). Though, in person, Steve Alexander told me that he was acutely interested in accurate visual communication. For this very reason he liked to explore the boundaries between design and fine art. Occasionally, in information designs such as Grundini's (Peter Grundy's), similar approaches are taken where strong colours and consistent shape seem to make light of heavy content. However, the designer has knowingly used what he describes as "approachable graphics" to draw the viewer in to engage with the content. In any case, in information design, the viewer may discern more easily that the graphics have an illustrative or explanatory role beyond decoration.

Figure 40: The new punk?, Mecha Fetus Visual Blog poster by Paul Robertson

Figure 41: Niedlich by Eikes Grafischer Hort

Elsewhere, a wider trend of decoration is evident in architecture and industrial design. Wallpaper is also experiencing new-found popularity. Busy backgrounds and ornamentation, the bane of the modernists, returned with a vengeance in the first decade of the 21st Century, especially in graphics and interiors:

> Ornament is clearly an integral part of the dominant visual language of the moment. The extent to which it has resonated with the public at large can be judged by the ubiquitous presence in the homes of Habitat-shoppers of the Toord Boontje filigree light shade. In Copenhagen, an entire hotel was redesigned from the inside out, as part of a Volkswagen-sponsored initiative called Project Fox. The carpets, wallpaper and furniture now teem with the kaleidoscopic explosions and fantasy pattern-scapes created by a group of designers and illustrators selected by the trend-conscious Berlin-based design publishers Die Gestalten. In Barcelona, too, the Maxalot Gallery has commissioned designers such as Hideki Inaba, Joshua Davis, eBoy and Rinzen to create a collection of wallpaper designs that, as they put it, 'celebrates the re-birth of wallpaper'. (Twemlow, 2001)

A hundred years ago Adolf Loos in *Ornament and Crime* said that decoration represents backwardness or even a degenerative tendency. What would re-attract the design world, if not the wider world to decorative design? A desire for celebrity, following on from the deconstructionist period of visual design where the designer was at last given a modicum of fame, does not in itself explain the excessive aesthetic, only the impulse to self-expression. The role of art directors and the ways in which they reflect the taste of the reading and viewing public should not be underestimated. Rinzen, for example, were pursuing successful enough careers in corporate design studios, but it was their unique approach to 'remixing' the illustrations made within their collective that was seized upon by magazine designers and ultimately propelled them on their heady illustration trajectory. A combination of other cultural ingredients has also led to this unprecedented point in design history: a celebration of low culture, the post-modern decontextualising of everything via the remixing method of design (these designers cut, share and paste because the technology enables such practices), a zeitgeist with an appetite for all things hand-made (including graphics) and a generation of visual practitioners weaned on 1970s visuality recently coming of age: As Albert Camus said, "A man's work is nothing but this slow trek to rediscover, through the detours of art, those two or three great and simple images in whose presence his heart first opened" (L'Envers Et L'Endroit, 1958, p.33).

Figure 42: Rinzen's Go Your Own Way exhibition in Barcelona, 2008, was: "celebrating the sexy scariness of chaos and mystery" according to the exhibition publicity. Art becomes wallpaper showing 70s influences: The George Harrison-like figure and the Hipgnosis/Hardie prismatic light beams, and visual echoes of the Push Pin Studio.
The title of the exhibition shares the name of a 1970s Fleetwood Mac song

The context for such designs, rather than one precisely defined in a communication design brief, might be globalisation: In a world where we have access to and are inundated by a huge range of visualities, this cornucopic design might be an honest visual reaction to those incoming messages. Rinzen apart (whose Rilla Alexander always provides a back story for her character designs), many other young design practitioners studiously ignore any distinctions between design and art, commercial commissions and self-expression. This often results in their work floating free of any contextual anchor. For those looking for meaning, the work seems only to point to itself and to other enigmatic examples that avoid direct reference to the globalised panorama which may have conceived them.

However it arrived, the compulsion for self-expression through design means that where there is no carefully targeted message to transfer, there is no need for clarity. This, combined with a reaction to a visually hyperactive world, might be enough to explain these excessive and obscure graphics.

It is difficult for a designer or critic seeking meaning in visual communication not to see this whole milieu as hopelessly noisy, regardless of whether it is a function of a furiously busy world or not. In *Obey the Giant*, Graphic design critic Rick Poynor opines: "Our triumphant age of plenty is riddled with darker feelings of doubt, cynicism, distrust, boredom and a strange kind of emptiness" (p.79). Put another way, "We have reached Utopia and it sucks", according to Richard Tomkins, Consumer Industries Editor of the Financial Times (2000). These graphics seem to reflect that we have available to us everything, here and now. Is this visual heaven or hell? The difficulty finding the designerly purposes of this work lies in the lack of articulation by the practitioners as to why it's done. Like artists, these designers don't have to tell us a thing. This certainly seems to be Poynor's difficulty with some of the bright young things of Australian design, Designiskinky (DiK):

> At this point in its life, DiK is perhaps poised between two kinds of activity. The friendly, non-critical tone and regular features such as a gallery of personal mugshots sent in by site visitors suggest something sociable, inward-looking, cliquey and not especially serious. But the site's intention to act as a forum and participate in a global design discussion also implies wider responsibilities and, if it's to be convincing, a commitment to higher standards of thinking and presentation [...] Every so often there are signs of frustration, too. 'I feel that a lot of the older generation Australian designers ... are actively destroying our international design abilities,' says Justin Fox in a DiK interview. 'We seem ashamed of our design work and this is so wrong.' [...] If the aim is to sharpen perceptions of young Australian design and encourage real debate – and not simply to provide yet another occasion for self-referential 'celebration' – then a more critically aware approach is essential. (Poynor, "Instant Content", 2002)

While we can't assume these new illustrators don't know what they are doing, there is something in Poynor's critique in that we also can't assume a thorough grounding in the history, contexts and science of visual communication if these practitioners seem incapable of articulating their own motivations and methods. To be fair though, noone before them has clearly articulated the affects of illustration.

A brief sample of these new illustrations shows that contemporary design has the potential to make the world a visually noisier place; a place where colour and sound no longer have associated meanings. Where clutter and repetition in single pieces of design, let alone across the gamut of burgeoning work, negate contemplative space, where pictorial design reflects no function other than that of selling itself and where its form shows avoidance or ignorance of aesthetic proportion, though seemingly not for any political reason, designs may be consistently presented in pretty, candy colours. One sees the fetishisation of the images of sex and war, combined with a rejection of the communicative power of colour, line and shape. It is as if, to accentuate the fashionable aspects of these visuals, subdued colours have become 'last season', and bright, candy colours of every hue are the new black! If we look upon this work as art, we can see these visuals as the work of artists expert, not in the traditional media of paint and clay, but in the application of advertising and pop-culture tropes. These illustrators are the heralds of the end of the economy as we have known it, signalling the final excesses of visual culture in the name of consumption. The Rinzen mural (Figure 43) looks uncannily like someone fiddling while Rome burns: the quintessential symbol of decadence. It is impossible and unhelpful to halt the stampede of wild illustration (as opposed to illustration tamed for a purpose). Doing so might curtail exciting new ways of visual explanation being accidentally discovered. To return momentarily to the verbal/textual parallels with pictures, an audience may just plain enjoy looking at different ways of seeing, and 'getting' what the artist is showing them, in the same way that readers enjoy new authors of fiction and their ways of describing. Criticising either won't stop such work from happening or from finding a receptive audience somewhere. The creation of pictures for the sake of it, or perhaps in the hope that a folio will be selected by an art-director or client, might however, lead to the devaluation of the design process: The art-director or the client choosing the style becomes the party making the design decisions as each artist pursues their own style. In this sense, much of the new illustration carries on exactly where deconstruction left off: the designer is less concerned with visually literate decisions about the function of the graphics in the context of the message, but rather pursues his or her own idiom leaving the art director or client to make the visual choices, that is, which designer/illustrator to use on this particular job, and the viewer to find meaning. These graphics may honestly speak through their cosmopolitan styles of being overrun by globalisation, but it could be argued that they in turn add to this graphic noise and accelerate it in a centrifugal cycle. Another valid response to noise might be to try and turn it down. Patrick Thomas seeks to do just that through his work. He explained to me that his approach is a deliberate response to what his contemporaries are doing. When vector graphics were popular in the early 2000s, he chose to work with photographic source material. When the popular style included polychromatic, complex illustrations, he expressed himself through one or two-colour, tone drop-out, hard-etched pictures on stark backgrounds. For Thomas, a simple graphic execution directs the reader to the idea rather than the visual surface. What started as a pragmatic approach to meet tight news deadlines became a signature style for his art without clients.

Figure 43: This graphic (detail), constructed as a team-effort by Rinzen, ran over four pages of an issue of *neomu* magazine

Looked at another way, under another label, much of the new illustration could legitimately be discussed as art. Doing so would frame it in a context where it no longer needs to explain itself. It's impossible to know whether this new approach becomes the dominant paradigm for illustration or whether, like deconstruction before it, it is a blip in the continuum. While it should never be said that illustration or any design must be undertaken following a prescriptive set of rules, it would certainly help communication to understand that there are good psychological and sociological reasons for employing illustration to communicate effectively when the intention is to confidently impart a message from one party to another. This communication will be all the more resonant if the illustrator understands more fully that certain colours and shapes do have certain associations and effects; that a reduction in certain details is likely to elicit a particular response. Otherwise, in the face of the next cycle of fashion when illustration falls out of favour, how do these practitioners argue for its importance? Rinzen told me that they are very sensitive to the fact that illustration can be a slave to fashion. Steve Alexander says that the lack of a brief, or the expectation of the client that "you will do what you always do" can be limiting and frustrating. As Max Bruinsma has said, "For the responsible designer, the 'anything-goes'-idea can turn out to be as paralysing as it may have seemed liberating at first sight. A reaction to this aesthetic 'free-for-all' may be the return to the established knowledge of the trade" (1997, p.4). Hopefully, since the 'established knowledge of the trade' has been lacking with regard to pictures, another valid reaction to the 'free-for-all' may be a desire to find out more about how pictures communicate. This may help establish a new base from which picture making exploration and experimentation can be made.

Augmenting visual literacy

As mentioned, a strategy to raise visual literacy is the showing of examples to pupils. This strategy is endorsed by Fransecky and Debes (1972) and Wileman (1993), but, according to Mallan (1999), who asks what visual literacy is ultimately for, "Students will not become 'readers' and more rounded individuals with a heightened sense of social responsibility and awareness simply because well-intentioned teachers 'immerse' them in picture books" (p.200). As I have just shown, some examples may, in any case, be counterproductive for the raising of visual literacy, where their creators are not interested in imparting specific messages and instead set out to confound audience expectations. Anne Bamford in her *Visual Literacy White Paper* declares 'awareness of intentionality' to be an indicator of visual literacy. With such an end in view, much of the new illustration is not exemplary at all, since it has no 'intention' in a conventional design sense. Bamford tries to add something substantial to this stand-by strategy: The showing of examples may prove very useful in promoting visual literacy if combined with critical analysis. Bamford phrases this strategy in the following terms: "Visual literacy includes critical knowledge. This is best developed through exposure to interesting and varied images and through thoughtful and thought-provoking questioning and discussion" (2003, p.5). This has been my intention in the previous discussion.

Bamford declares that, "There can be no dictionary of meanings for the symbols of visual communication [...] visual communication is made up of presentational symbols whose meaning results from their existence in particular contexts" (2003, p.3). To this end she has carefully devised a table which can be applied to all pictures (see Appendix D). This strategy attempts to cover the social interaction implicit in using pictures to communicate. However, perhaps because of the social focus, the visual system of the viewer is not really a consideration in Bamford's table. Noone in the visual literacy arena has directly addressed the importance of what the eyes and brain do to solve the visual problems of the real world. At a stretch perhaps realism and its alternatives might be read into Bamford's criteria: For example, at point two against 'Issues': "How is the way the issue is shown in the image similar to or different from how you see this issue in the world?"; her point two against 'Information': "What information has been included and what information has been left out?"; and points one and six against 'Persuasion': "Why has a certain media been chosen"; "How has the message been affected by what has been left out or is not shown?" This last question echoes both Goldsmith's and Gombrich's findings that the most realistic picture is not the most communicative, and Wileman (1993, p.120) who proposed the following question as a criterion regarding 'Visual Design Considerations': "Does the visual contain only the essential information?" However, it would be of benefit to ask overtly under 'Information', in light of what I have demonstrated in this book, "what degree of pictorial realism is used in this picture and why?" As I have aimed to show, this question is of fundamental importance to the ways a picture can communicate.

Bamford's table details some useful questions planned to help ascertain the 'intentionality' of a picture. However, questions such as 'why has a certain media been chosen', or 'what information presented is factual/manipulated/framed?' do not prompt an understanding of the physical operations of vision. Rather, these questions work in the same way as Lupton and Miller's problematising of interpretation, and take vision itself for granted. As long as visual literacy competencies are prompted and described in these terms, teacher and student are relying only on shared or dissimilar cultural understandings of pictures and the visual instincts of the picture maker. A combination of strategies which make a problem of both the psychology and sociology of vision would seem best, in light of what I have ascertained in the previous two chapters, to help explain and improve visual literacy. At the very least a discussion can ensue which seeks to find out where and why individual approaches might be appropriate. Visual literacy concepts should include the knowledge of what the visual system responds to and what it is on the look out for. The discussion in the second chapter of this book revolved around understanding the workings of the human visual system. If that understanding is to be applied for picture-making it should also, in theory, be applicable to critically analyse existing pictures.

In such a capacity I use that understanding now to show the strengths of a range of illustrations and diagrams. What my analyses of these pictures have in common is an evaluation of each picture's relationship to realism.

Having established an expansion in the boundaries for visual literacy strategies, based on the aspects of pictures that I have so far identified, I now provide further clarification of my theory through a critical appraisal of exemplars of picture-making. Each example will throw light on the aspects of vision that I have so far studied in the book in an attempt to put into practice Christopher Crouch's (2008, p.195) idea of "treating visual literacy as an active process" and developing it "so that it involves a critically analytical reading of visual texts". I will examine exemplars of high visual literacy as they pertain to my criteria of reductions in realism, and in steps decreasing in realism along the continuum. In accord with the findings in Chapters 1, 2 and 4, I will concentrate firstly on pictures that are photographic or highly realistic, then on pictures which comprise silhouettes, then those which invoke perceptual constancies, and on to those which draw on gestalt closure for their effects. Within these broad categories I will comment on pictures that; are realistic; de-identify their subject but are otherwise realistic; show the loss of interior detail—the picture functions through silhouette or detailed outlines only—; are exemplars of line drawing with interior detail (Since the line drawing as a mode of rendering is consistently shown in Goldsmith's review to be the most communicative, I will give it special attention here); and those that show where picture meets type.

Exemplars chosen along the continuum

The realistic picture

This book may seem in many ways to be a treatise against realism, but this is not the case. I hope a more accurate description would be that it argues against the over-use of realism. Photographs can be, of course, highly effective in visual communication. The issue of specificity alluded to in the previous chapter can be made positive in the appropriate circumstances. When we see a photo of a specific person, it really is recorded light, reflected off that real person; a copy, as close to the real thing as possible in two dimensions, of an actual person. Photography then is an entirely appropriate communication medium if the intention is to document that specific person; likewise, for places. Frank Zachary (editor of 1940s magazine, Holiday) followed a very particular approach, called 'environmental portraiture', which plays to these core strengths of photography (Heller & Pomeroy, 1997, p.46) by capturing a specific person in their typical, identifiable habitat. A photograph is also particularly good at capturing texture in a way that communicates viscerally to the viewer. Food and drink and their freshness are well portrayed by crisp and clear photography. In this sense, a photograph comes close to allowing the viewer to 'assess' the food in a manner similar to a customer looking at produce in the marketplace.

However, in situations where a person photographed is an actor or 'talent' for a commercial, photography's impossible task is to get real, specific people to fit the generic role they are assigned: young mortgagee, sensible retiree, and so on, cast such that they do not draw attention to their 'otherness'. This application of pictures grows ever more tenuous and suspect as each part of the world becomes more multicultural and multiracial. As I have shown in Chapter 4, in photography's 19th century infancy, practitioners were concerned precisely with photography's inability to avoid being specific. While this argument regarding photography's 'proper' place in visual culture has long been played out, the design community (especially advertising design) has continued regardless.

De-identified subjects

A simple inversion of a realistic picture will break an immediate connection with the reality to which it referred and allow for transmission of a different message. The example at Figure 44 is produced following the method used in Sports Tonight, a news segment on Australian television. The show's designers have hit upon an ingenious way of getting the most from existing video footage: Through inversion the pictures are both precise and generic at the same moment. Following this process, the players in the picture become unrecognisable to the viewer who must instead begin to look at what activity is taking place in the picture. Specificity is a problem with photography when the meaning of the picture does not benefit from specifics. For example, a picture of footballer David Beckham, in a news context may be problematic since his image is not only synonymous with football but also with merchandising and even celebrity gossip. If the picture is meant to capture something about football, rather than a specific sports-celebrity, the photograph of that specific person begins to be less than ideal for the intended task.

Figure 44: Simply making a negative image from a positive will make the subjects difficult to identify, thereby directing viewer attention away from identity toward the action depicted

Subjects may also be de-identified and made more generic through cropping. Iranian posters have recently received some long-overdue recognition. In my view, if we can generalise about them at all, what makes them special (apart from the striking Farsi calligraphy) is their approach to image. Unlike the use of photography for design practised in the west, Iranian poster imagery seems deliberately obscure. The pictures themselves tend to offer glimpses rather than a good look at whatever is captured. In the poster at Figure 45 by Ali Khorshidpour we see a bird wing rather than a complete bird. Counter-intuitively, this focus suggests more about flight than a complete bird would. In other words, this detail can evoke something other than the specific creature to which it belongs. Only an ornithologist could identify the specific bird from its wing. The layperson has to find meaning elsewhere in such a picture: it is about the wing, and wings are about flight. This allows other interesting aspects of photography to come to the fore, such as its ability to sharply render textures and vivid colours as interesting compositional elements within themselves. Since most western critics have, again, concentrated on the typography evident in these works, I sought the opinion of one of Iran's celebrated graphic designers, Pedram Harby, about why parts of the photographs are obscured or removed. I wondered, was this approach following on from an Iranian art tradition? Harby responded, "In Iran we have always been told that the use of religious personalities' pictures are not allowed or suitable. That is one of the reasons that you barely see the use of such pictures. The techniques gained from these restrictions become methods to apply to other kinds of pictures".

VISUAL LITERACY AND PICTORIAL STRATEGIES

Figure 45: Ali Khorshidpour's approach is to use photographic realism while avoiding representation (Medley after Khorshidpour)

Of course, this tradition is not simply a restriction on artistic expression but a complex set of cultural parameters which able designers have long happily worked within. The visuality built over centuries through the denial of representational pictures is not about to collapse under the weight of the 'new' medium of photography. Egyptian graphic designer and calligrapher, Ahmed Moustafa further explains the prominence of abstraction over realistic representation in the Islamic arts as a function of history:

> You cannot say these scientists [Arab scholars translating and expanding on the drawings and schema of Plato, Euclid, etc.] in botany, mathematics, medicine piled up such a body of knowledge with the notion of not being able to draw. But in the 10th century Ibn Muqlah, the great scribe and translator, made the theory of proportional Arabic script, based on Euclidean theory [...] So it is inconceivable that the artist will go back and portray the outer shell of that reality'. (Daines, 1996, p.10)

Depictions of the unreal

Since a paradox is at the heart of this book—that one may communicate more accurately through less accurately rendered images—it seems fitting that one of the most appropriate uses for realism is for the depiction of the unreal. In the first-person, point-and-click computer game, Exile, for example, the realism in texture mapping and lighting effects helps provide, in an otherwise outlandish environment, a sense of immersion for the game-player (Figure 46). Importantly, the makers did not include human figures in the computer modelling[3], but instead keyed in video clips of real actors.

Figure 46: Vividly rendered, hyper-real 3D design (by Seth Fisher, Stephen Hoogendyk, Ron Lemen, Francis Tsai) from the computer game, *Exile*, (Presto Studios) creates an immersive visual experience of a non-existent world

In the picture below, the illustration is realistic enough to help suspend disbelief for a moment, but shows enough painterly texture for that suspension to be immediately questioned. In this regard, its rendering is deliberately 'real'. The artist has chosen the degree of realism. This picture, despite its almost photorealist nature is all about graphic shape. It is the nightmarish 'cape' and 'horns' and the absence of light in a large portion of the picture—that this shape can barely be contained in the frame of the picture—that creates such a powerful sense of foreboding. The fact that in reality these are harmless creatures is only of secondary relevance. Even a great white shark would look much less threatening to the reader when s/he turned the page to arrive at this double page spread advertising outboard engines. The atypical viewing angle accentuates the drama of the fish's shape. The fisherman's unknowing hand on the gunwale adds to the sense of vulnerability (Figure 47).

---

3. Realistic humans that also evoke empathy in the viewer are notoriously difficult to achieve in 3D modelling. The quest for 'perfect' computer modelled humans paradoxically has lead to cadaverous apparitions in the gaming and filmic realms. This problem of unwanted viewer revulsion can be plotted in part of a graph termed the 'Uncanny Valley'; a graphical trough named by Japanese roboticist, Matsuhiro Mori in his *Bukimi no tani* (The uncanny valley) (1970).

VISUAL LITERACY AND PICTORIAL STRATEGIES

Figure 47: Painted illustration for outboard motor advertisement by Akira Yokoyama. In spite of the detail in the picture, the graphic shapes propel the meaning and emotion of this design

Caricature

A highly realistic picture captured by a photograph may be distorted using the computer to create a caricature, but a caricature may also be made using the less realistic line drawing. However, it is difficult to conceive of a caricature being developed within a drawing of any less detail than this since caricature drives towards making clear the difference between objects of the same class (to solve the homogeneity problem) while distillation or the removal of identifying details works ultimately towards making objects within the class appear generic.

Figure 48 is an advertisement for women's boots in which a woman's legs are exaggerated to provide a startling break with realism, to refute any notion that this picture is about a specific person (the face would more likely be foregrounded in such a case) and to accentuate the subject of the advertisement. The "spotlight" psychology I discussed in Chapter 2 is at work here with the designer having performed the spotlighting on the viewer's behalf. In effect, this is a caricature of the boots, to show that they are big and chunky (compared to the norm of women's footwear) and to simultaneously distinguish them from those by other makers.

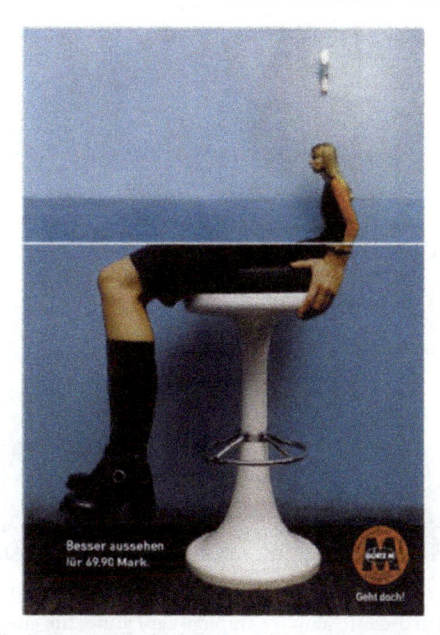

Figure 48: Editorial advertisement for boots in which the designers have performed the 'spot-lighting' on behalf of the reader. Design: Stephan Ganser/Hans Jürgen Lewandowski. Photography: Axl Jansen

In my introduction, I cited Poracsky, Young and Patton who complain that pictures are assumed to be unimportant in education, "It is almost as though the educational system is seeking to wean the student's mind off graphics by climaxing in books that are all words and no illustrations" (1999, p.107). One thing we might do is to look at the imagery available in a society where this 'weaning away' does not occur. What can design from Japan, where grown men in business suits read comics on the way to work, show us about caricature? In Japan the mainstream cinema is anime or animated film rather than 'live action' film, and this phenomenon in itself is worthy of consideration. One of the many noticeable attributes of such film is the way in which character's faces, even in the more serious of these works, may be momentarily (and perhaps even grotesquely, to unaccustomed western eyes) stretched into an embarrassed grin, an angry scowl or a hearty laugh in order to give primacy to the emotion being expressed. The more general nature of the emotion rather than the specificity of the character seems to be of prime importance in these fleeting moments, and Japanese visuality seems to have just the right techniques to communicate this (Figure 49).

Figure 49: Miyazaki's *Porco Rosso* shows the Japanese tendency to momentarily obscure a character's specifics in order to amplify, through caricature, the emotion of the moment

Silhouettes

Realistic outlines without interior detail

Typically, pictures drawn as silhouettes can be seen in instructional graphics for any tasks ranging from assembling furniture to self-defence messages: these often comprise comics that are largely picture-driven, as they need to work across linguistic barriers for globalised wares, and for depicting instructions that would be difficult to intellectualise from text back into an action that is physical and visual. Generally speaking, such comics depict accurately scaled figures and aspects of the appropriate environment in outline, but disregard most of the interior detail of these. The airline safety card, for example, is created to reinforce the message of the flight attendant's safety demonstration. These cards are largely graphic for quick comprehension and multi-lingual understanding. The illustrations on the cards show realistically proportioned figures and aspects of the aeroplane environment in outline but avoid depicting their interior details. This approach, exemplified in the Lufthansa card at Figure 50 achieves a number of objectives. First and foremost it highlights through colour the important information in each frame. The reduction in detail allows colour to come to the fore.

As Rick Poynor suggests of this style of graphic in his chapter *Blank Look*, "If it has an aesthetic character it is one that has arisen from the modest aim of giving only as much visual information as is needed to convey the basic facts. Anything more elaborate would slow down a potentially urgent message" ("Obey the giant", 2001, p.78). Happily for Lufthansa, the gold colour of its logo also works well as a highlight colour demanding attention. The absence of colour and uniformity of outline in the human figures defuses any sense of emotion that would be attached to such situations in reality. At the same time the realistic proportions suggest a serious and matter-of-fact directness for the message.

Figure 50: Lufthansa safety card: Colour focuses attention on specific points, the outline drawings focus attention on operational instruction

The airline safety card makes clear the object of attention and its operation by allocating the limited colour to only these aspects of the design. Meanwhile, the outline-only characters deny recognition: Airline passengers need not and cannot ask who these figures are, so must ask themselves instead, what are these people doing?

Figure 51: Steff Geissbuhler's *Peace*, 1985, is a welcome exception to the 'weaning off' from the apparently childish delight in anthropomorphism

Steff Geissbuhler's Peace poster (Figure 51), was chosen by curators Elizabeth Resnick, Frank Baseman and Chaz Maviyane-Davies for their exhibition and book, *The Graphic Imperative* (2005). The poster was designed to commemorate the 40th Anniversary of the bombing of Hiroshima. The picture encourages reconciliation between two "giant" nations, Japan and the U.S.A., symbolized, hilariously and ironically in the two modern-day, low-brow myths, Godzilla and King Kong gazing lovingly into each others eyes while strolling hand-in-hand into a new dawn. Geissbuhler includes just enough information in the silhouettes to allow identification of the creatures, and to show their heroic and monumental stature via a low vantage point.

Another powerful example from the same exhibition catalogue is the *iRaq* poster by Forkscrew Graphics (Figure 52). Its silhouette references the famous iPod publicity but also shows that what we visually recall of the tormented Abu Ghraib prisoner, Professor Ali Shalah, is his forced stance in stark graphic outline. Every seasoned logo designer knows the importance of the silhouette to viewer retention.

PERCEPTUAL CONSTANCIES

Figure 52: Forkscrew Graphics, *iRaq*, 2004, is a gruesome parody of the well-known iPod silhouettes

Perceptual constancies

Line drawings with interior detail

Since the category of line drawings was consistently demonstrated in Goldsmith's review of illustrative experiments to be the most communicative, I will explore some of the potential of line drawing in more depth. In Hergé's *Tintin* we see realistic settings peopled with iconic characters. The backgrounds—street scenes, railway stations, airports and ships—are executed with vivid precision; Hergé, after a time, even employed an illustrator, Bob de Moor, specifically to draw these backgrounds. Often the source material for his visual fiction was photographically captured from the real world to be meticulously copied in pen and ink. McCloud sums up this approach to picture making:

> Storytellers in all media know that a sure indicator of audience involvement is the degree to which the audience identifies with a story's characters. And since viewer-identification is a specialty of cartooning, cartoons have historically held an advantage in breaking into world popular culture. On the other

hand noone expects audiences to identify with brick walls or landscapes and indeed, backgrounds tend to be slightly more realistic. In some comics, this split is far more pronounced. The Belgian 'clear line' style of Hergé's Tintin combines very iconic characters with unusually realistic backgrounds.

Hergé makes very clear this separation between 'cartoon' characters and precision drafting in the background drawings, especially of architecture (street scenes, actual edifices such as the Geneva train station, and so on). Scott McCloud succinctly describes this separation between character and background as if it encourages a kind of role-playing while reading: "one set of lines to see. Another set of lines to be" (p.43).

Interestingly, Hergé never once drew more than a medium close-up of Tintin. Tintin may be judged by what he says and what he does, not on his looks, which, apart from the famous quiff, are an assemblage of anti-caricature features. Tintin's travelling companions, Captain Haddock, Professor Calculus and company are, by contrast, strong caricatures which may be judged by their appearance as much as their deeds. Tintin displays his traits – loyalty, bravery and intelligence – through action and speech. The distance the artist kept from his creation in each panel and the distilled drawing of this character are ideal to present these attributes.

However, this separation is not used to foreground the characters at the expense of the background. The lack of shadow in Hergé's line-drawing encourages careful inspection of the backgrounds; yes, they are objectified (in the sense of rendered objectively) but these drawings prompt viewing and evaluation of the background in a way a photograph of a real place never would. Often in Hergé, it is only the lines that explain where there is a corner, of a building for example, or the edge of the pavement. To 'read' the pictures in *Tintin* the lines must be carefully examined. The photograph, and even a realistic drafting that includes light and shadow and accurate colouring would allow the background to be taken for granted, and to read the characters as travelling across, in front or on top of this background. This is never the case in Hergé. The background is meant to be read objectively but never taken for granted. Every line communicates something and is painstakingly drafted. Moreover, the line work in these 'backgrounds' appears to be (though in truth is not) of a consistent weight, giving the drawings what Scott McCloud describes as a democracy of form (1993). In the terms of my Chapter 2, this line work technique promotes a gestalt sense of belonging among the details so rendered: They are accorded the same level as each other in the visual hierarchy of the picture.

Another European comics artist, Italian, Milo Manara, works with detailed and accurate line drawings to create surreal picture narratives. The accurate line drawing, like the very realistic picture, seems to cleave closely enough to visual reality to create powerful subversions of that reality when the artist chooses to do so. According to Mitchell (2008), "any picture may become a metapicture, whenever it is employed as a device to reflect on the nature of pictures" (p.19). Manara's reflected cayman drawing (Figure 53) from his comic *The Great Adventure* (1988) can be described as such: This picture is remarkable for drawing to our attention the way that water reflects light, and the ways it does not. Seen from a low perspective on a river, moon and boat are, reasonably, reflected across the horizon. The cayman being much 'closer' to the view-point should not be reflected across the horizon but across the plane where its body intersects with the water. Sound effects certainly should not be reflected at all! But Manara cleverly draws the reader's attention to the fact that the comic is a visual medium only and that everything within that medium is under the control of the artist.

Figure 53: Manara's illustration sets the matter-of-fact presentation of line drawing against surreal content and composition: Everything in the picture is reflected across the horizon where only the boat should be shown this way

Gestalt closure

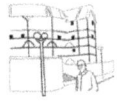

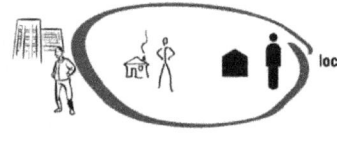

Gestalt understanding of colour and shape and closure

As Scott McCloud has eloquently observed, action in comics actually takes place between frames and within the mind of the reader (1993). His subtitle for *Understanding Comics* is *The Invisible Art*, for this reason. The implication of this observation is that a complete distillation of image down to nothing can still be meaningful so long as good clues are given either side of the picture: The 'missing' image, which will be different for each reader/viewer, is part of a sequence. Any comic will demonstrate this happening, but few, I believe will do so as eloquently as Milton Glaser's *Red Chair Painted Yellow* (Figure 54). Glaser's removal of any character or 'actor' from the scene emphasises that the action does indeed happen only between the frames in comics. The clues he leaves are perfect: the paint pot and the red chair changing frame by frame, daub by clumsy daub until the final scene has the chair defined only by its shadow on the floor and the wall at its back.

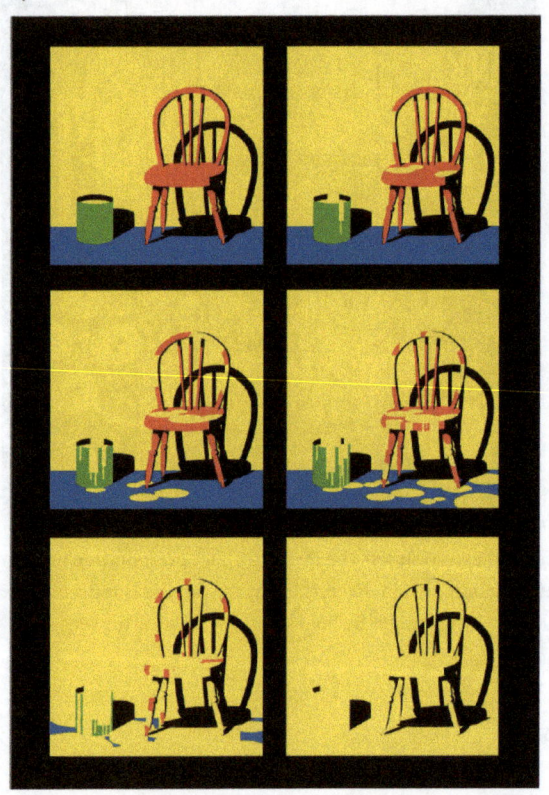

Figure 54: Glaser's *Red Chair Painted Yellow* clearly relies on closure by the reader: The 'action' occurs in between the frames (Medley after Milton Glaser)

Ryan Pequin's comic at Figure 55 shows closure, or lack thereof, on the obscured speech bubble, suggesting a refocusing on behalf of the central character, away from the words of his associate, and on to the cup he holds in front of him. It puts the aural into the visual realm in such a way as we can imagine the sound being 'turned down' as if it were part of a soundtrack. Instead of being replaced by other sounds or music as we might anticipate in film, it is replaced by a mute visuality. In this sense it is another metapicture, describing as it does some of the unique potential of a comic panel where the aural is slave to the visual, and disturbing closure to affect a pansensual understanding of a strictly visual medium.

Figure 55: In the last panel here, Ryan Pequin buries the 'aural' aspects of his comic (*The Walk*) under the visual, in effect turning down the sound

Comics appear in a vast range of visual styles but nearly all have in common that they reduce the detail of the visible world in terms of texture and colour, and they typically employ outlines to describe objects. In addition, they often exaggerate physical differences between characters, utilizing some of the methods of the caricaturist. Each of these techniques would seem to play to the predilections of the eye and brain, and explain at least some of the appeal of comics' visual environments.

Where picture meets type

Integral/NORM's design for Köln-Bonn airport is significant in terms of this zone along the realism continuum where pictures come closest to type (Figure 56). Intégral's design for the wayfinding program at the Köln-Bonn Airport in Germany employs two basic shapes (with subtle variations to each) not only to make up the pictograms—somewhat lyrical versions of typical airport graphics—but also the unique typeface for the airport (by NORM Typographers). Thus, type and pictures are expressed through the same set of rules creating the basis for an extraordinarily coherent wayfinding program. In addition, Integral has thoroughly explored the idea of corporate identity and decided that a logo may vary from time to time, or department to department, within a corporation without detriment to the overall personality of the corporation. In this way, the aforementioned icons are put to work, each with the addition of some colourful but deliberately misregistered fill to create identities for different services within the airport. These fills lend humour and ironic warmth to the otherwise unemotional icons. At the same time the whole program becomes design *about* design but not at the cost of communication with its intended audiences. In the terms set out in this book: a masterpiece of visual literacy.

Figure 56: Integral/NORM's design for the Köln-Bonn airport show type and picture built from the same components

E-mail sign offs are, by contrast, a vernacular, non-expert use of graphics from this picture/type point on the realism continuum. Yuki (et al) explains that, "depending on an individual's cultural background, facial cues in different parts of the face are weighted differently when interpreting emotions" (2005, p.303). This weighting finds expression in type-as-picture within e-mail sign-offs or emoticons:

> Emoticons are combinations of certain keystrokes that combine to form an approximate facial expression, which can be used to convey the emotional state of the writer. For example, in the United States the emoticons :) and :-) denote a happy face, whereas the emoticons :(or :-(denote a sad face. However, Japanese tend to use the symbol ^_^ to indicate a happy face, and ;_; to indicate a sad (or crying) face (Pollack, 1996). Consistent with our hypothesis, the Japanese emoticons for happiness and sadness vary in terms of how the eyes are depicted, while American emoticons vary the direction of the mouth.

The Japanese approach seems to derive from an e-mail author's personal experience of emotion rather than simple observation of emotion: When one smiles, one can feel the lower eye-lid crinkling upwards though this may not be so obvious in another (Figures 57 and 58). This accords with Dondis' and de Sausmarez's notion of 'body-felt' understanding of forms in space.

∧ ∧   ▪   ▪
—   /—/

Figure 57: Typical Japanese emoticons emphasise the eyes

:)   :(

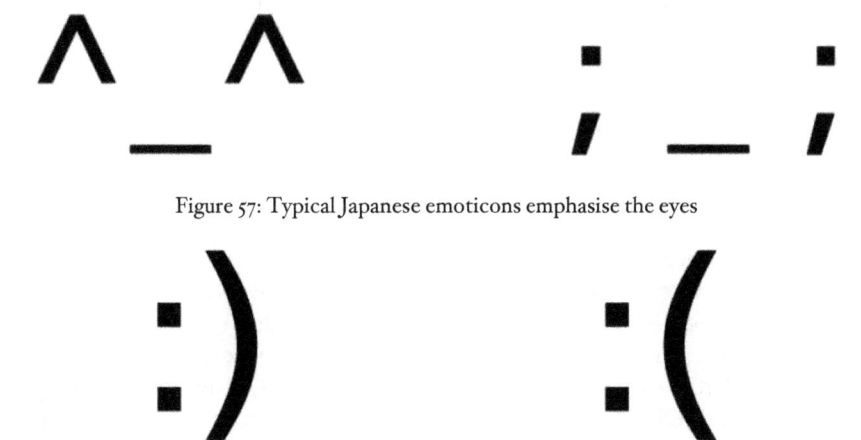

Figure 58: Typical US emoticons emphasise the mouth

Type is picture

According to Spiekermann and Ginger, "nobody has ever classified typefaces according to their problem-solving capabilities" (1993, p.57). My research provides the capacity to point design theory in that direction. Here I will discuss the ways in which, I believe, my research on pictures can be applied to type.

As Gregory explains in *The Intelligent Eye*, when the eye and brain take in images and try to understand them, the brain is continuously testing object hypotheses. These hypotheses are matched, presumably, against a 'vocabulary' of existing objects in memory. Similarly, as the eyes and brain learn to read, progressing past the stage of having to look at every letter, having to sound out every word, words themselves pass into this storehouse of existing shapes and the reader begins to read by word shape: Words become visible objects with a clearly identifiable shape. Gestalt psychology, used to describe how images are apprehended, is also completely applicable to type: Gestalt psychology is implicit (though never named) in type theory in terms of word spacing versus line spacing. The spacing between letters must never be larger than the gaps between words; and the gaps between words may never be so loose as to be larger than the gaps between lines (leading) as this confuses the reader as to the direction of reading; should it be left to right or top to bottom? According to gestalt theory, objects (in this case letters) that are close together, are thought of by the human visual system to belong together. Further, sets of words, especially common phrases that often fall together on to the page have unique and memorisable shapes. A simple self-test can be undertaken if one reads two versions of the same paragraph, one set in sentence case and another all in upper case. The upper case will take longer to read and seem more difficult. This is because there are no unique word shapes in uppercase text: each word is of uniform height, and each has become a rectangle, roughly speaking. With all-upper-case text, the reader is reduced to reading in the manner of their early attempts: letter by letter, word by word.

Of course things are learned through experience, but these learned things must slot into pre-existing abilities and are enabled by such abilities. It is clear that we must learn in order to read. But what we are born with is the ability to understand that a group of black shapes (for example, on a piece of paper) clustered together and separated out from similar groups by a space appear to belong together. This is one of the reasons typography must conform to visual rules of gestalt in order that we know what to read next. The type historian will gladly explain that words were not always separated from each other in the Phœnician, Greek, Etruscan or Latin alphabets, but that the literate could nevertheless read text. However, lines were always separated to aid reading, and, eventually users of the written languages came to realise that doing the same between words would improve readability.

Words, when printed on a page, are pictures. In this sense then lies the possibility of teaching both graphic design aspects, type and picture, with the same pedagogical approach. As we get closer to abstract forms such as text, the same attributes that hold text together as a typeface (shape and 'line' weight) begin to come to the fore for pictures. I showed the example of the Integral/NORM Köln-Bonn identity, where type and picture are made from the same 'building blocks' as just such an example of these qualities.

While post-modern design has seen the 'free-for-all' use of pictures and type whenever the designer decided, cognitive psychology provides for a more dependable relationship between design and message. Some knowledge of synaesthesia, for example, tells us sharp shapes shouldn't be used to promote a friendly message, nor should rounded shapes and bright colours be used to promote negative or sombre messages unless there is a knowing reason for doing so.

In addition, both type and picture may be examined as departing from a norm. The concept of caricature can be a new design structuralism: that which does not depart from a norm (the Norm) is the exnominated: the unstated to which all other things are compared and by which all other things are recognised. In the case of type it is not inconceivable to think of Helvetica as the 'norm' for sans serif typefaces. In comparison to this norm we can easily observe that a typeface such as Microgramma seems horizontally stretched or extended (Figure 59). In another instance, small differences can be exaggerated to highlight differences between typefaces (Figure 60).

Mitchell (2008) has described:

> the dialectic between word and image as an unsurpassable fissure or fold in the fabric of representation, but one which is always "widening" or being "overcome" in the practical use of signs or symbols at any time. So words and images have always "converged" in the phenomenology of writing as a visible, graphic notational scheme that unites eye and ear, symbolic, iconic and indexical elements. (p.28)

Choice of font has a visual aspect that can (depending upon how far away the type is from 'what we read most' as Licko would have it) draw attention to itself or not. The example Mitchell gives is religious illuminations, where the word is meant to be 'seen but not read'. A designer might describe such letterforms somewhat more prosaically, merely as a 'display face'. In both definitions it is a form that is drawing attention to itself as something other than the main text. In this sense, such a form has departed from the norm of lettering. Mitchell's is a historical example, but we might classify type today by its distance from Helvetica (for sans serif fonts) or from Times (serif fonts). This is a radical departure on how to teach type but makes sense in terms of this book. I am not suggesting that there exists a perfect norm. In this sense this is not an Internationalist approach. People read best what they read most, no typeface is necessarily more easily classified as legible than another: Just as norms for human faces are personal and unique though people in a shared culture or location might experience strong correlations.

For too long type has been categorised by a particular method simply because noone has asked "why classify it this way?". Why not classify it by shape? Shape is a better method since classifying by period is fraught with problems: how can we be confident about the period when it is easy for the post-modern type designer to ape a previous period? Rounded, on the other hand, at least in synaesthetic terms, is always approachable and friendly (Bang, 1991). Given that type is about communicating to an audience and the audience is unlikely to be versed in the development and history of type, why not classify type in a way that both the designer and their audience can understand? A way more akin to how a design audience reacts to things, that is, a way of classifying type more in tune with psychology and sociology; by shape first, association second, and history last.

As I have shown, many visual literacy theorists lament that written language is regarded as a means to a higher form of thinking than the visual. But, to be literate and to be visually literate can be the same thing in graphic design, or, at the very least, steps along the same journey since words, and the letters that make them up in printed form, *are* pictures. Choice of font can work in the same way as the many things so ably described in the theories of Kepes and Dondis, right through to Frey and Fisher: symmetry, of contrast in Bodoni for example, versus the dynamic stress of the humanist fonts; the sharp, dangerous looking points of Koch Fraktur versus the open, approachable geometry of Futura (Figure 61).

Figure 59: Caricature of Microgramma letterform using Helvetica as the norm

Figure 60: Caricature of Arial letterform using Helvetica as the norm

Figure 61: Synaesthesia (in this case using the visual to suggest experience from the tactile world) could be an unorthodox, but nevertheless effective, means of classifying type

Conclusions

Graphic design theory has been very much typo-centric. On the rare occasions where discussion had centred on the non-textual elements of graphic design it tended to focus on composition rather than the execution of an image. The prevalence of photographic pictures in design's 20th Century history was never a result of sound perceptual reasoning. Likewise, the pursuit of photo-realism in 3D modelled animation is an unimportant direction for visual research or practice. Pictures which, on the other hand, distil and abstract reality can take advantage of the human visual system's need and ability to make sense of the noisy images presented to it by the real world. Accordingly, I have quoted those theorists outside of the design fields who had attempted to quantify pictures in order to find out how they communicate. These were found in art history, psychology and in a group of educational theorists gathered loosely under the term 'visual literacy'. A shared concept of some of the theorists from these disparate disciplines is the 'realism continuum'. Though this concept was not ideally articulated in the literature for my purposes, the notion of different levels of realism causing different responses in the viewer has been central to my argument. With regard to how images are received by a viewer, I hope I have demonstrated that there is a difference between realistic pictures and pictures that are distilled or abstracted away from realism. I have explored how the less realistic pictures can be perceived in the first place, and that these pictures might actually be understood more directly by the human visual system. In order to understand the visual world around it, the mind must have ways of recognising aspects of that world that do not rely on precise views of objects. The same object can never be seen from exactly the same angle twice. Therefore, recognition of things in the world is not bound by a perfect match between a memory of things and their actual appearance. Instead we judge the appearance of things against mere mental schema, unconcerned with exact size, shape, colour or orientation. It is this fact that allows illustrations, of varying degrees of fidelity, to remain communicative in spite of their departure from the way things look in reality. In some cases these illustrations better match those mental schema than does a specific object.

The realism continuum is best thought of as helping us to understand two major tasks of the human visual system. At its abstract end the continuum model helps designers to choose pictures which best solve the object constancy problems for the audience. Designers and illustrators should know that objects typical to a class are the easiest for their audience to learn and then recall. At the realistic end, the continuum model assists in the task of solving the homogeneity problem: which specific example of person or thing is the audience being asked to recognise? Between these two ends of the continuum, line drawings seem to be in a cognitive 'sweet spot'. Perhaps because these drawings seem to mimic aspects of visual perception itself, they seem to be appropriate for a wider range of tasks than the very concrete or the very abstracted image. As graphic designers and visual communicators, we can begin to experiment, with research grounding, to make pictures which play directly to the psychology of vision: using invariants which acknowledge perceptual constancies; and thinking about the realism continuum as a measure to tell us when we are trying to distinguish *between* classes of objects or *within* a class of objects, and therefore when to accentuate the synaesthetic, gestalt or caricature approaches that drawings afford us. In other words, visual communicators can help solve the visual problem of realism on behalf of their audience rather than relying unquestioningly on photography; a medium that tends to re-present the complex visual problem of the visible world.

The realism continuum concept also shows that information designs, including diagrams, ideograms and pictograms, can be placed conceptually on the same spectrum with more detailed and expressive drawings in spite of the separation of these modes of representation in design literature. In turn, this has the effect of including illustration in the set of visual tools available for serious visual communication, rather than, as it is talked about in much of the trade and in education, a whimsical practice; a cousin of fine art. These descriptions have had the effect of placing illustration as, at best, a cryptic and mysterious activity devised to inspire different feelings and meanings in each viewer, and at worst, a self-indulgent past-time, rather than the powerful communicator it can be. Of course, the makers of one kind of picture are not necessarily going to be good at making the other, nor feel inclined to make them. Illustrators need to, if they are to be good at what they do, pursue a particular style until they have unlocked and mastered their own particular way of seeing and visually describing the world. However, I hope that this book strengthens arguments for employing illustrators for more communication tasks. In that sense it is aimed at designers and art directors. These professionals are at complete liberty to peruse any photographed and drawn pictures from the high-fidelity colour photo through to pictograms to locate the most appropriate picture for the task at hand. Goldsmith (1984, p.69) explained that being visually literate means having the ability to respond to pictures as equivalents of the objects they represent. However, armed with the knowledge developed through this book, designers can aspire to escape this narrow definition. They have the ability through picture choice and construction of diagrams to suggest links and relationships that do not exist as visible objects in the real world. Some important aspects of visuality are concerned precisely with rendering visible those things that are not 'objects' to begin with but relationships between visible objects. Visual literacy as a definition then, might be augmented to include the ability to make visible those concepts which are invisible in reality.

I stated at the outset that I was less interested in the role of interpretation for the understanding of the pictorial aspects of design. My bias has been adopted for the purposes of imparting intentional messages: can there be a consensus on the ways pictures communicate because of their relationship to realism? This focus by no means limits discussion of the picture in design to psychology but also allows for social applications of graphics. However, I have no doubt that, whether visually literate or not, the viewer of any graphic design focuses their visual system through powerful cultural and experiential lenses. It may even be the case that the more visually literate the reader the more interpretive and less mechanical is their understanding of an image. Just as reading text becomes a seemingly effortless task built upon innate physiological abilities but is also a highly structured task based on cultural codes, so it may be that the reading of pictures will be improved, as many of the visual literacy lobby suppose, through greater practise. I have tried to show that there can be some shared understanding of how pictures communicate as a function of their realism quotient. Of course we must learn things through experience, but these learned things must slot into pre-existing abilities and are enabled by such abilities. The fact that a caricature of a specific person can be widely recognized, and that the synaesthetic, Bouba/Kiki experiment elicits an almost perfect consensus of cross-modal cognition, even between vastly different cultures, suggest that aspects of visual experience can be shared, even when the pictures used are derived from different ends of the realism continuum.

Evaluating pictures according to their communicative potential is a worthy challenge in spite of warnings that it is a wild-goose-chase. As I explained in the introduction to this book, design theorists need to be clear about the distinction between *images* and *pictures*, that the vocabulary we seem to be questing for in a useful design theory is not about images but about ways of capturing images in pictures. *Pictures and type* should be the focus of our design theories more than *images and words*. If this has been the reader's first foray into picture theory allied to design, I heartily recommend the Swiss Design Network (including Scheuermann, Joost and Schneller) who have done a great deal to divorce visual rhetoric from the assumptions that it is subordinate to verbal rhetoric. If the reader is interested in the semiotics of visual 'grammar', I highly recommend the comics analyses of Thierry Groensteen who questions and dismisses many of the assumed parallels between textual and pictorial language. While the work of visual theorists, such as Kress and Van Leeuwen, who allied pictorial communication to linguistics has been invaluable in bringing picture theory into academia in general and design discourse in particular, it is high time to recognise that the picture in design needs its own place. Theories that are founded in linguistics and literature should be treated with scepticism when applied to pictures. Text lacks the simultaneity and immediacy of pictures. Certainly there is no direct equivalence to be found in literature or linguistics to the realism continuum; a key to understanding pictures and putting them to work in deliberate visual communication.

This book can not cover all contingencies of pictorial communication. Graphic design theory is a contested space. Debate regarding typography was wide-ranging and vigorous during the 20th Century. A debate of equal import must happen around pictures in design, and in order for it to happen, those interested in design need to gain an awareness of the few arguments in the field. Reflecting upon their understanding of these, designers and critics will be able to add to the discourse surrounding pictures and their use in deliberate communication. By extension, such articulation will also enable the designer to communicate more confidently with his or her client about all aspects of visual communication, rather than just the typographic half of the graphic design equation. Visual literacy theorists recommend the showing of examples to students in order to improve visual competence. However, the explanation accompanying exemplars, and not just the intent of the image maker, also makes the examples effective. The words to explain and accompany these visuals, and the reasons for choosing particular examples in the first place are precisely what the research for this book has provided. This book may not change the way designers design. However, it may give to those designers the words to help persuade their clients that they are paying for expertise in visual thinking and not just unusual ways of seeing. If nothing else, I hope that this book can be the irritating grain of sand that might help build a pearl of picture theory for designers and design theorists.

References

Abdullah, R. and Hübner, R. (2006). *Pictograms, Icons & Signs*. London: Thames and Hudson.

About (n.d.). Retrieved October, 2007 from E-boy website: http://hello.eboy.com/eboy/about/

Agar, M., Bermejo, R., Giner, J.A., Goertzen, J., Green, P., Grimwade, J., Gude, K., Holmes, N., Lacava, L., Lertola, Mill, J., J.,Munk, O., Parsonson, C., Peltzer, G., Rorock, G., Schwochow, J.,Serra, J., Sims, G., Tavejnhansky, L., Urabayen, M. & Velasco, J. (2003). The best infographics in history. In J. Arrea (Ed.), *Malofiej, 10th World Infographics Awards* (pp.35-53). Pamplona: Capitulo Español.

Albarn, K. & Miall Smith, J.(1977). *Diagram: The Instrument of Thought*. London: Thames & Hudson.

Allesi, S. M., & Trollip, S. R. (1991). *Computer-Based Instruction: Methods and Development* (2nd ed). New Jersey: Prentice Hall.

Arnheim, R. (1954). *Art and visual perception: A psychology of the creative eye*. Berkeley: University of California Press.

Art of the Book (2006). On-line video, retrieved, May, 2008, from 92nd St Y.: http://www.92y.org/shop/category.asp?category=888Podium%5FVideo888

Ausburn, L. & Ausburn, B. (1978).Cognitive styles: Some information and implications for instructional design. *Education Communication and Technology Journal*, 26(4), 337-354.

Ausburn, L.J. & Ausburn, F. B. (1978b). Visual literacy: Background theory and practice. *Programmed Learning and Educational Technology 15*. 291-297.

Ausburn, L.J. & Ausburn, F. B. (1994). A cross-cultural perspective on visual literacy: Challenges for technical communicators. *STC Proceedings* 445-447.

Bamford, A. (2003). *The Visual Literacy White Paper*. Sydney: Adobe Systems.

Bang, M. (1991). *Picture this: How pictures work*. New York: Little Brown and Company.

Barthes, R. (1974). *S/Z*. London: Cape.

Barthes, R. (1982). *Camera Lucida*. New York: Hill and Wang.

Bello, F. (1953). The Information Theory, in *Readings in Management Information Systems*, G. B. Davis & G. C. Everest (Eds.). New York: McGraw-Hill Book Company, 23-32.

Berger, J. (1974). *Ways of Seeing*. Middlesex: Penguin.

Berlo, D. K. (1960). The Process of Communication. New York: Holt, Rinehart and Winston, Inc.

Boenhert, J. (2006). *Emotion Graphics*. Retrieved November, 2006 from Eye Magazine: http://www.eyemagazine.com/feature.php?id=134&fid=606

Bonsiepe, G. (2002). Some Virtues of Design. *Proceedings of Design beyond Design Symposium* (pp.1-26). Maastricht: Jan van Eyck Akademie.

Bonsiepe, G. (1997). *Interface - an approach to design*. Maastricht: Jan van Eyck Akademie.

Bosshard, H.R. (2000). *Der Typographische Raster*. Zürich: Verlag Niggli.

Brennan, S.E. (1985). The caricature generator. Leonardo, 18(3) (pp.170-178).

Bringhurst, R. (2004). *The Elements of Typographic Style*. Vancouver: Hartley & Marks.

Bruinsma, M. (1997). Learning to read and write images. *Eye Magazine, 25*(7), 3-4.

Bruinsma, M. (1997). A rhetoric of images. *Eye Magazine, 27*(7), 3.

Buchheit, M. (n.d.). *Simplifying the Complex*. Interview with Nigel Holmes, Information Designer and author of Wordless Diagrams. Retrieved March 15, 2008 from Spotlight, Volume II, Issue I: http://www.creativerefuge.com/pages/spotlight5.htm

Camus, A. (1958). *L'Envers Et L'Endroit*. France: Editions Gallimard.

Clarke, D. (1995). *The Rise and Fall of Popular Music*. New York: St Martin's Press.

Crouch, C. (2008). Afterword. In J. Elkins (Ed.), *Visual Literacy* (pp.195-204). New York: Routledge.

Daines, M. (1996). Ahmed Moustafa. *Baseline, 21*, 9-16.

Debes, J. (1969b). The Loom of Visual Literacy. *Audiovisual Instruction, 14* (8), 25-27.

Dondis, D.A. (1973). *A Primer of Visual Literacy*. Cambridge, Massachusetts: MIT Press.

Dwyer, F. M. (1972). *A guide for improving visualized instruction*. Pennsylvania: Learning Services, State College, PA.

Dwyer, F. (1979). The communicative potential of visual literacy: Research and implications. *Educational Media International Vol 2*, 19-25.

Digital Humans. (1996, March), [advertisement] *Wired*, 4.03, 65.

Dondis, D. A. (1973). A Primer of Visual Literacy. Cambridge, Massachusetts: MIT Press.

Dwyer, F. M. (1972). *A guide for improving visualized instruction*. Pennsylvania: Learning Services, State College, PA.

Dwyer, F. (1979). *The Communicative Potential of Visual Literacy: Research and Implications*. Educational Media International, 2, 19-25.

Eden, J. (1978). *The Eye Book*, Penguin, Middlesex, England

Ekman, P. (1985). *Telling lies*. New York, New York: W.W. Norton.

Elam, K. (2004). *Grid systems: Principles of organizing type*. New York: Princeton Architectural Press.

Elkins, J. (2008). *Visual Literacy*. New York: Routledge.

Errea, J. (2003). Essential infographics, an interview with John Grimwade. In J. Arrea (Ed.), *Malofiej, 10th World Infographics Awards* (pp.5-18). Pamplona: Capitulo Español.
Eysenck, M.W. (2004). *Psychology: An International Perspective*. Sussex: Psychology Press.
Fantz, R. (1961). The origin of form perception. *Scientific American,* 204, 66-72.
Feldman, E. (1976). Visual literacy. *Journal of Aesthetic Education,* 10(3), 195-200.
Fernandez, S. (2006). The Origins of Design Education in Latin America: From the HfG in Ulm to Globalization. *Design Issues 22* (1), 3-19.
Fischer, F. & Hiesinger, K.B., with Fukai, A. (Eds.).(1994). *Japanese design, a survey since 1950*. Philadelphia: Philadelphia Museum of Art.
Fransecky, R.B. & Debes, J.L. (1972). *Visual literacy: A way to teach a way to learn*. Washington D.C.: Association for Educational Communications and Technology.
FreshRMX (n.d.). Retrieved January, 2008 from Rinzen: http://www.rinzen.com/?id=360 retrieved 4.9.2005
Fussel, D. & Haaland, A. (1978). Communicating with Pictures in Nepal: Results of Practical Study Used in Visual Education. *Educational Broadcasting International,* 11(1), 25-31.
Geipel, J. (1972). *The cartoon: A short history of graphic comedy and satire*. Newton Abbot: David and Charles.
Geisler, W.S. & Diehl, R.L. (2002). Bayesian natural selection and the evolution of perceptual systems. *Phil. Trans. Royal Society. Lond. B, 357,* 419-448.
Gibson, J.J. (1971). The information available in pictures. *Viewpoints 47*(4): 73-95.
Giorgis, C., Johnson, N.J., Bonomo, A., Colbert, C., et al (1999). Visual Literacy. *Reading Teacher, 53*(2), 146-153.
Goldsmith, E. (1984). *Research into illustration: an approach and a review*. Cambridge: Cambridge University Press.
Gombrich, E. (1982). *The Image and the Eye*. Oxford: Phaidon.
Gombrich, E. (2002). *Art and Illusion*. Oxford: Phaidon.
Gooch Erik Reinhard Amy Gooch Perception-Driven Black-and-White Drawings and Caricatures Bruce UUCS-02-002 School of Computing University of Utah Salt Lake City, UT 84112 USA January 22, 2002
Green-Lewis, J. (1996). *Framing the Victorians, photography and the culture of realism*. Ithaca: Cornell University Press.
Gregory, R. L. (1970). *The Intelligent Eye*. London: Weidenfeld and Nicholson.
Gregory, R. L. (1977) Knowledge in perception and illusion. From: Phil. Trans. R. Soc. Lond. B (1997) 352, 1121–1128.
Groensteen, T. (2007) *The System of Comics*. Jackson: University Press of Mississippi.

Gropper, G. L. (1963). Why is a picture worth a thousand words? *AV Communication Review*, 11, 75-79.

Grundmann, U. (2001). *Intelligence of vision: An interview with Rudolf Arnheim.* Retrieved July, 2006 from Cabinet: http://www.cabinetmagazine.org/issues/2/rudolfarnheim.php

A Guide to Color Separation (1995). *Digital color prepress volume two Agfa prepress guide.* Mortsel, Belgium: Miles Inc. and Agfa-Gavaert N.V..

Hall, S. (1980). Encoding/decoding. In Centre for Contemporary Cultural Studies (Ed.): *Culture, Media, Language: Working Papers in Cultural Studies, 1972-79* London: Hutchinson, pp. 128-38

Hardie, G. (2005). Drawing—My Process. In L. Duff and J. Davies (Eds.). *Drawing—The Process.* Bristol and Portland: Intellect.

Heller, S. (1993). *Cult of the Ugly*, Retrieved December, 2004 from Eye Magazine: http://www.eyemagazine.com/feature.php?id=40&fid=351

Heller, S. (1999). Graphic Design Magazines: Das Plakat. *U&lc, 25*(4).

Heller, S. & Arisman, M. (2000). *The Education of an Illustrator.* New York: Allworth Press.

Heller, S. (2000). The object poster: Word+image=impact. In G. Swanson (Ed.), *Graphic design and reading: An uneasy relationship* (pp.137-140). New York: Allworth Press.

Heller, S. & Pomeroy, K. (1997). *Design Literacy.* New York: Allworth Press.

Haddad, H. (2005). The Design and Effect of Character/Agents in Computer Mediated Interactive Experiences. PhD Thesis, Department of Design, Curtin University of Technology, Western Australia.

Heller & Arisman (2000). *The Education of an Illustrator.* New York: Allworth Press.

Heller & Arisman [2004] *Inside the Business of illustration*, Allworth Press

Helmholtz, H. von 1866 Concerning the perceptions in general. In Treatise on physiological optics, vol. III, 3rd edn (translated by J. P. C. Southall 1925 Opt. Soc. Am. Section 26, reprinted New York: Dover, 1962).

Hochberg, J. & Brooks, V. (1962). Pictorial recognition as an unlearned ability. *American Journal of Psychology 75.* 624-628.

Hollis, R. (1994). *Graphic design: A concise history.* London: Thames & Hudson.

Hubel, D. & Wiesel, T.N. (1962). Receptive fields, binocular interaction and functional architecture in the cat's visual cortex. *Journal of Physiology. 160*, 106-154.

Hyland, A. & Bell, R. (Eds.).(2001). *Pen & Mouse.* New York: Watson Guptil.

Hyland, A. & Bell, R. (Eds.).(2003). *Hand to Eye.* London: Laurence King.

Idato, M. (2000, July 18). Matt Groening's family values. *The Age* (Melbourne, Australia).

REFERENCES

Jock Kinneir + Margaret Calvert (n.d.). Retrieved October, 2007 from Designmuseum: http://www.designmuseum.org/designinbritain/jock-kinneir-margaret-calvert

Janser A & Junod B (Eds.): *Corporate Diversity*. Baden: Lars Müller Publishers; 2009:10-20

Johnson, W. L., Rickel, J. W. & Lester, J. C. (1999). Animated Pedagogical Agents: Face-to-Face Interaction in Interactive Learning Environments (2000). *The International Journal of Artificial Intelligence in Education*, 11, 47-48, Retrieved: March, 21, 2003, from http://www.csc.ncsu.edu/eos/users/l/lester/www/imedia/papers.html

Jones, J. and Seenan, G. (2004). *The camera today? You can't trust it. Hockney sparks a debate*. The Guardian, 4 March 2004.

Joost, G & Scheuermann, A (2006). Design as rhetoric: basic principles for design research in *Drawing new territories*, Proceedings of the Swiss Design Network Conference, 2006

Julian Opie: Signs (n.d.). Retrieved November, 2007 from http://www.indyarts.org/julianopie/information.html

Kepes, G. (1944). *Language of Vision*. Chicago: Paul Theobald and Company.

Kiefer, B.S. (1995). *The Potential of picturebooks: From visual literacy to aesthetic understanding*. New Jersey: 1995 Prentice-Hall Inc.

Kiefer, B.S. (1995). *The Potential of Picturebooks: From Visual Literacy to Aesthetic Understanding*. New Jersey: Prentice-Hall Inc.

Kinross, R. (1989). The Rhetoric of Neutrality. In V. Margolin (Ed.). In *Design Discourse: History, Theory, Criticism* (pp.131-143). Chicago: University of Chicago Press.

Kirby, T. (Producer/Director). (2007). *The Genius of Photography* [Video]. London: BBC

Klanten, R. & Hendrik, H. (Eds.). (2005). *Illusive*. Berlin: Die Gestalten Verlag.

Klanten, R. & Hendrik, H. (Eds.). (2007), *Illusive 2*. Berlin: Die Gestalten Verlag.

Koda, T. & Maes, P. (1996). Agents with Faces: The Effects of Personification of Agent. *Proceedings of HCI'96*, London, Retrieved: November, 6, 2001, from http://www.media.mit.edu/-tomoko/docs/HCI_final.doc.ps

Knowlton, J. (1966). On the definition of a picture. *AV Communication Review* 14, 147-183.

Kress, G. & Van Leeuwen, T. (1996). *Reading images: The grammar of visual design*. New York: Routledge.

Licko, Z, VanderLans, R., with Gray, M. (1993). *Emigre, the book: Graphic design into the digital realm*. New York: Van Nostrand Reinhold.

Loos, A. (1997). *Ornament and crime: Selected essay*s. Riverside, California: Ariadne Press.

Luke, A. (1994). *The social construction of literacy in the primary school.* Melbourne: Macmillan.
Lupton, E. (1989). Reading Isotype. In V. Margolin (Ed.), *Design discourse: History theory criticism* (pp.145-156). Chicago: University of Chicago Press.
Lupton, E. & Miller, J.A. (1999). *Design Writing Research.* New York: Phaidon.
Malamed, C. 2009. *Visual Language for Designers.* Beverly, Massachusetts: Rockport.
Mallan, K. (1999). Reading(s) beneath the surface: Using picture books to foster a critical aesthetics. *Australian Journal of Language and Literacy 22*(3), 200-211.
Manara, M. (1988). *The great adventure: The adventures of Giuseppe Bergman* (J. Surbeck, Trans.). New York: Catalan Communications.
Mareis, C. (2005). Illustration—an attempt at an up-to-date definition. In R. Klanten and H. Hellige (Eds.), *Illusive* (pp.4-5). Berlin: Die Gestalten Verlag.
Mareis, C. (2005). Illustration in practice. In R. Klanten and H. Hellige (Eds.), *Illusive* (pp.8-9). Berlin: Die Gestalten Verlag.
Markey, D. (Director). (1992). *1991, the year punk broke* [Video]. USA: Geffen Pictures.
Mau, B. (2004). *Massive Change.* London: Phaidon.
Mazzucchelli, D. (2009). Asterios Polyp. Pantheon Books, New York.
McAlhone, B. & Stuart, D. (1998). *A Smile in the mind.* London: Phaidon Press Ltd.
McCloud, S. (1993). *Understanding Comics, the Invisible Art.* New York: HarperCollins.
Medley, S. (2008). Less Realism: More Meaning. Evaluating Imagery for the Graphic Designer, PhD Thesis, Faculty of Education and the Arts, Edith Cowan University.
Medley S. (2009) The feeling's neutral for pharmaceutical packaging: how the pharmaceutical aesthetic equals the Modernist aesthetic. *AMJ* 2009, 1, 10, 36-43. Doi 10.4066/AMJ.2009.59
Meggs, P.B. & Purvis, A.W. (2006). *Meggs' History of Graphic Design.* New Jersey: John Wiley & Sons.
Meggs, P. (1992). *Type and Image.* New York: Van Norstrand Reinhold.
Mitchell, W.J.T. (2008). Visual Literacy or Literal Visualcy? In J. Elkins (Ed.), *Visual Literacy* (pp.11-29). New York: Routledge.
Mirzoeff, N. (1999). *An Introduction to Visual Culture.* London: Routledge.
Mitchell, W.J.T. (2008). Visual Literacy or Literal Visualcy? In J. Elkins (Ed.), *Visual Literacy* (pp.11-29). New York: Routledge.
Modley, R.(1976). *Handbook of Pictorial Symbols.* Mineola, New York: Dover Publications.
Mori, M. (1970). Bukimi no tani [The uncanny valley]. (K. F. MacDorman & T. Minato, Trans.). *Energy, 7*(4), 33–35.

Morris, C. (1938). Foundations of the Theory of Signs vol 1. *International Encyclopaedia of Unified Science*. Chicago: University of Chicago Press.

Morton, J. & Johnson, M.H. (1991). CONSPEC and CONLEARN: A two-process theory of infant face recognition. *Psychology Review, 98*, 164-181.

Müller, L. (2000). *Josef Müller-Brockmann, Pioneer of Swiss Graphic Design*. Baden: Lars Müller Publishers.

Müller-Brockmann, J. (1983). *The graphic artist and his design problems*. Zurich: Verlag Niggli.

Neurath, O. (1946). *From Hieroglyphics to Isotypes*. London: Nicholson and Watson

Neurath, O. (1973). From Vienna Method to Isotype. In M. Neurath & R.S. Cohen (Eds.), *Otto Neurath, empiricism and sociology* (pp.217-240). Dordrecht and Boston: D.Reidel

Nikolajeva, M. & Scott, C. (2006). *How picturebooks work*. New York: Routledge c/- Taylor & Francis.

Nodine, C. F., Locher P. J. & Krupinski, E. A. (1993). The Role of Formal Art Training on Perception and Aesthetic Judgment of Art Compositions. *Leonardo* 26 (5), 219-227

O'Shea, R. P., Govan, D. G., & Sekuler, R. (1997). Blur and contrast as pictorial depth cues. *Perception, 26*, 599-612.

Pendle, G. (Winter 2006/07). *Otto Neurath's Universal Silhouettes*. Retrieved June, 2007, from Cabinet: http://www.cabinetmagazine.org/issues/24/pendle.php

Philpot, R. (2000). Unreal Actors to Invade Film Sets. *The Australian IT*, Tuesday September 5, 55.

Popper, K.R. (1959). *The Logic of Scientific Discovery*. New York: Basic Books.

Poracsky, J., Young, E. and Patton, J.P. (1999). The Emergence of Graphicacy. *The Journal of General Education, 48*(2), 103-110.

Poynor, R. (2001). *Obey the giant: Life in the image world*. London: August Media Ltd.

Poynor, R. (1991). *Typography Now*. London: Booth-Clibborn Editions.

Poynor, R. (1998). *Typography now two: Implosion*. London: Booth-Clibborn Editions.

Poynor, R. (2002). *Instant content*. Retrieved May, 2005 from Eye Magazine: http://www.eyemagazine.com/critique.php?cid=206

Preble, D & Preble, S. (1994). *Artforms: An Introduction to the Visual Arts* (5th ed), New York: HarperCollins College Publishers.

Ramachandran, V.S. & Hubbard, E.M. (2001b). Synaesthesia: A window into perception, thought and language. *Journal of Consciousness Studies, 8*(12), 3 - 34.

Rand, P. (1991). From Cassandre to Chaos. *AIGA Journal of Graphic Design*.

Rathgeb. M. (2006). *Otl Aicher*. London: Phaidon.

Rauschenberger, R. & Yantis, S. (2001). Masking unveils pre-amodal completion representation in visual search. *Nature 410*, 369-372.

Resnick, E., Baseman, F. and Maviyane-Davies, C. (Eds.). (2005). *The graphic imperative: International posters for peace, social justice and the environment 1965-2005*. Boston: Massachusetts College of Art.

Rhodes, G. (1996). *Superportraits: Caricatures and recognition*. East Sussex, England: Psychology Press.

Rivers, C. (2004). *Maximalism*. Brighton: Rotovision.

Robertson, B. (1995, March). 3D Characters on Parade. *Computer Graphics World: Animation for Television*, 17(3), 28-34.

Robertson, B. (1997, July). Virtual Humans at Work. *Computer Graphics World: Visualization*, 20(7), 33-39.

Rodman, L. (1985). Levels of Abstraction in the Graphic Mode. In D. E. Hickman, (Ed.), *Teaching technical writing: Graphics*, anthology No. 5, (pp. 1-9). St. Paul, Minnesota: Association of Teachers of Technical Writing.

Roska, B. and Werblin, F. (2001). Vertical interactions across ten parallel, stacked representations in the mammalian retina. *Nature 410*, 583-587.

Rowland, A (1990). *Bauhaus source book*. New York: Van Nostrand Reinhold.

Ruddigkeit, R. (Ed.).(2003) Introduction to *Best of German Commercial Illustration*
Mainz: Verlag Hermann Schmidt.

Samara, T. (2002). *Making and Breaking the Grid*. Gloucester, Massachussets: Rockport.

de Sausmarez, M. (2002). *Basic design: The dynamics of visual form*. London: A&C Black.

Schonell, F.J. (1932). *The essential spelling list*. London: Macmillan Education.

Schumann, J. T., Strothotte, T., Raab, A. & Laser, S. (1996). Assessing the Effect of Non-Photorealistic Rendered Images in CAD, CHI 96 Electronic Proceedings, Short Paper, Retrieved: August, 26, 2003, from http://www.acm.org/sigchi/chi96/proceedings/papers/Schumann/chi96fi.html

Seitz, J. A.(1998). Nonverbal metaphor: A review of theories and evidence. *Journal of Genetic, social, and general psychology monographs, 124*(1), 121-143.

Shannon, C. E. (1948). A Mathematical Theory of Communication (Based on original Bell System Technical Journal version), (1998, February 2 – last update), Retrieved: May, 11, 2001, from http://cm.bell-labs.com/cm/ms/what/shannonday/paper.html

Shaughnessy, A. (2006, October 15). *Graphic Design vs. Illustration*, DesignObserver. Retrieved January, 2008 from http://www.designobserver.com/archives/018460.html

Shaw, P. (1984). Tradition and Innovation: The Design Work of William Addison Dwiggins. *Design Issues, 1*(2), 26-41.

Shaw, B. (1969). *Visual symbols survey: Report on the recognition of drawings in Kenya*. London: Centre for Educational Development Overseas.

Showroom: Character Design (2004). *Novum Gebrauchsgrafik, 36*, (11) 4.

Skolos, N. & Wedell, T. (2006). *Type, image, message: a graphic design layout workshop*. Gloucester, Massachussetts: Rockport.

Sontag, S. (1977). *On Photography*. New York : Farrar, Straus and Giroux.

Sontag, S. (2004). What have we done? *The Guardian, May 24, sec. G2*, 2-5.

Spiekermann, E. & Ginger, E.M. (1993). *Stop stealing sheep & find out how type works*. Mountain View California: Adobe Press.

Stermer, D.(2000). Teaching Illustration.In S. Heller & M. Arisman (Eds.), *The education of an illustrator* (pp.97-101). New York: Allworth Press.

Stoichita, V. (1997). *A Short History of the Shadow*. London: Reaktion Books.

Thorgerson, S. (1978). *Hipgnosis: Walk Away René*. London: Paper Tiger/Dragon's World.

To See, Brain Assembles Sketchy Images, Eyes Feed It (2001). Retrieved April, 2004, from http://unisci.com/stories/20011/0329011.htm

Tomkins, R. (2000, December 16-17). We Have Reached Utopia—and It Sucks. *Financial Times, Weekend*, p.1.

Tschichold, J. (1995). *The new typography: A handbook for modern designers*. Berkeley: University of California Press.

Tufte, E. (1990). *Envisioning Information*. Cheshire, Connecticut: Graphics Press.

Tufte, E (1997). *Visual Explanations*. Cheshire, Connecticut: Graphics Press.

Twemlow, A. (2001). *The decriminalisation of ornament*. Retrieved October, 2005 from Eye Magazine: http://www.eyemagazine.com/feature.php?id=126&fid=553

Uddin, M.S. (1997). *Axonometric and Oblique Drawing*. New York: McGraw Hill.

Walsh, V. & Kulikowski, J. (Eds.). *Perceptual Constancy: Why Things Look as They Do*. Cambridge: Cambridge University Press.

Walters, J.L. (2001). "Gerard Unger". Retrieved November, 2006 from Eye magazine: http://www.eyemagazine.com/feature.php?id=4&fid=10 No. 40, 2001).

Warde, B. (2000). The Crystal Goblet. In G. Swanson (Ed.), *Graphic design and reading; An uneasy relationship* (pp.91-94). New York: Allworth Press.

Wertheimer, M. (1938). Laws of organization in perceptual forms. In W.D. Ellis (Ed.). *A Source Book of Gestalt Psychology*. London: Kegan Paul (pp.71-88).

Wileman, R. E. (1993). *Visual Communicating*. New Jersey: Educational Technology Publications.

Wileman, R.E. (1980). *Exercises in Visual Thinking*. New York: Hastings House.

Wilson, M. (1997). Metaphor to Personality: the Role of Animation in Intelligent Interface Agents, Animated Interface Agents: Making them Intelligent (in conjunction with IJCAI-97), Nagoya, Japan, Retrieved: February, 1, 2001, from http://www.dfki.uni-sb.de/imedia/workshops/anina.html#session1

Wlassikoff, M. (2005). *The story of Graphic Design in France*. Corte Madera, California: Gingko Press.

Wolfson, W. (2001). What Sticks: Robo Sapiens, Informationweek.com, Retrieved: December, 12, 2001, from http://www.informationweek.com/story/IWK20011120S0007

Wonisch, D. & Cooper, G. (2002). Interface Agents: Preferred Appearance Characteristics Based Upon Context. Virtual Conversational Characters: Applications, Methods, and Research Challenges in Conjunction with HF2002 and OZCHI2002, Melbourne, Australia, Retrieved: March, 21, 2003, from http://www.vhml.org/workshops/HF2002

Woodiwiss, A. (2001). *The Visual in Social Theory*. London: Athlone Press.

Wurman, R.S. (2001). *Information Anxiety 2*. Indianapolis: Que.

Yuki, M., Maddux, W. & Masuda, T. (2007). Are the windows to the soul the same in the East and West? Cultural differences in using the eyes and mouth as cues to recognize emotions in Japan and the United States. *Journal of Experimental Social Psychology 43*, 303–311.

Zwimpfer, M. (2001). *2D Visual Perception*. Zürich: Verlag Niggli.

© Copyright, Stuart Medley, 2011-2012

Index

A

Abdullah, Rayan 81, 83, *88*
abstraction (*see also* distillation) 12-30, 82-90, 112
ACG *see* Behage, Dirk; Bernard, Pierre; and Draaijer, Fokke
Aicher, Otl 29, 58, 73, 82, 83, 87
Albarn, Keith 84
Alexander, Rilla xi, 14, 100, 104
Alexander, Steve xi, 14, 70, 100, 101, 107
Annukka, Sanna *69*
anti-caricature (*see also* caricature) 120
Arisman, Marshall 13, 98
Arnheim, Rudolf 9, 10, 15, 40
Arntz, Gerd 81, 83
Art Nouveau 57
art-poster 68
Ausburn, L.J & F. B xvi, 96

B

Baines, Phil 4
Bamford, Anne 4, 107, 108
Bang, Molly 127
Barthes, Roland xiii, 18-20
Basel 60
Baseman, Frank xi, 118
Bauhaus 55-65, 73
Behage, Dirk *63*
Bell, Nick *64*
Bell, Roanne 68, 69
Berger, J 18, 19
Bernard, Pierre *63*
Bernhard, Lucien 20, 55, 57
Bill, Max 58
Billout, Guy 72

INDEX

Bley, Thomas xi
Bliss, Charles 82
Boehnert, Jody 99, 100
Bonsiepe, Gui 2, 19, 97
Bouba/Kiki effect 51, 52, 131
Brennan, Susan. 47
Bringhurst, Robert 5
Brody, Neville 65-67
Bruinsma, Max 2, 107

C

Calvert, Margaret 73, 83-84
camera 6, 7, 11, 18, 30, 49, 59-61, 79
Camus, Albert 103
caricature xiv, xvi, 46-53, 114, 120, 126, 130

  of colours *50*
  of faces 46, *48*, 49, 116, 131
  of landscape *50*
  of non-face images 49, 114, *115*, *128*

Carson, David 66
Cheuk, Deanne xi, 97
closure 41, *42*, 43, 46, 109, 121-123
composition 2, 4, 15-19, 57, 65, 77, 84, 111, *121*, 129
constancy *see* perceptual constancies
Constructivism 56, 57, 61, *63*, 64, 65, 68, 96
comics *42*

  closure in comics 122
  characters and realism 25, 41, 100, 120
  line art in comics *46*, 120
  and accessibility in information design 92
  airline safety cards 116
  and visual literacy 115, *121*, *123*, 132
  Understanding Comics

Crouch, Christopher. xi, 93, 96, 109

Crossville *100*
Crystal Goblet xv
Cult of the Ugly 76

D

Da Da 65
Debes, John 3, 107
Deconstruction 57, 61, 62-78, 98-106
decoration 58, 99, 101-103
Designiskinky 104
De Stijl 55, 56, 65
diagram xvi, 1, 6, 79-93
distillation 12, 24-29, 34, 36, 42-46, 52-57, 73-75, 79-85, 114, 120, 122, 129
Doesburg, Theo van 56
Dondis, Donis 3, 14-20, 27, 125, 127
Draaijer, Fokke *63*
drawing
Dwyer, Francis 23-30

E

eBoy 102
Eeshaun 100
Ekman, Paul 36
Elam, Kimberley 65
Elkins, James 134
El Lissitsky 56-57
e-mail sign offs *see* emoticons
Emily the Strange 100
emoticons 124-125
environmental portraiture 85, 109
Euclid 112
Exile game 112, *113*

F

Fantz, R.L 34
Fernandez, Silvia 58
Flash software 70, *71*

144

Forkscrew 118, *119*
Fransecky, Roger 3, 107
Freehand software 72
Fussel, Diana 29, 53

G

Geipel, John 49
Geissbuhler, Steff 118
Gestalt 15-19, 41-46, 58, 86-87, 109, 120-126, 130
Ghostboy 100
Gibson, J. J. 6-11, 21, 24, 40, 49
Glaser, Milton 10, *122*
Goldsmith, Evelyn 18, 25, 92, 108, 109, 119, 131
Gombrich, Ernst xiii, 8, 9, 12, 24-27, 38-41, 91, 98, 108
Gooch, Bruce & Amy 49, 53
Goodchild, John *50*
graphicacy (*see also* visual literacy) 3
Grapus *see* Behage, Dirk; Bernard, Pierre; and Draaijer, Fokke
Green-Lewis, Julia 10, 11, 89
Gregory, R. L. 8, 18, 25, 34, 40, 51, 125
grid 57, 58, 64-69, 81, 83, 87
Grimwade, John 81
Groensteen, Thierry 132
Gropper, G. L 23, 85
Gros, Jochen 83
Grundini *see* Grundy, Peter
Grundy, Peter xi, 86, *90*, 101
Gubbles, Sharim 100

H

Haaland, Ane 29, 53
Haddad, Hanadi xi, 27, *28*
Haslam, Andrew 4
Harby, Pedram xi, 111

Hardie, George xi, xiii-xiv, *42*, 86, 103
Hello Kitty 100
Henderson, Hazel 91
Hergé 41, 119-120
Heller, Steven 4, 13, 20, 55, 57, 76, 85, 109
Hellige, Hendrik xvi, 72, 96
hieroglyphics 82
high-fidelity 7, 79, 131
Hipgnosis 72, 103
Hockney, David 10
Hollis, Richard 56, 58, 75
Holmes, Nigel *74*, *80*
homogeneity problem 30, 36, 52, 53, 114, 130
Hubbard, Edward 51-52, 101
Hubel, D. & Wiesel, T.N 45
Hübner, Roger 81, 83, *88*
Hyland, Angus 68, 69

I

Ibn Muqlah 112
iconic pictures 25-30, 79, 83-85, 90, 97, 100, 120
ideogram 130
illustration

commercial art 9, 68, 97
fashion 59, 70, 74, 96
new illustration 68-74, 96-107
Pop Art 98

illustrator

Education of an Illustrator 4, 13
Illustrator software 72

image

definition of 4-9

infographics *see* information design
information architecture *see* information design

information design. 29, 67, 73-93, 130
information graphics *see* information design
Integral (design studio) 73, 123-126
International Style *see* Neue Scweizer Grafik
interpretation. 10, 17, 19, 20, 30, 51, 92, 108
Iranian posters. 111

J

Japanese animation (anime) 115, 116
Jarvis, James 100
Janser, Andres 60
Joost, G & Scheuermann, A (2006). 19, 132
Junod, Barbara 60

K

Katsumi, Masaru 82-83
Kepes, György 15, 17, 41, 127
Khorshidpour, Ali 111, 112
Kiefer, B.S 27
Kinneir, Jock 73, 83-84
Kinross, Robin 29
Klanten, Robert. xvi, 72, 96
Knowlton, James 23, 85
Köln-Bonn Airport 73, 123-126
Kress, Gunther 19, 132
Kugler, Oliver *50*

L

Licko, Zuzana 127
line
   line drawing 53, 70, 109, 114, 117, 119-121, 130
   line weight 120, 126

Loewy, Raymond 75
Loos, Adolf.. 103
low-fidelity pictures.. 7, 26, 28
Lupton, Ellen 2, 17-20, 42, 59, 61, 90, 92, 108

M

Maddux, William 124
Maldonado, Thomas 19, 83
Maholy-Nagy, Laszlo 56, 65
Maholy-Nagy, Lucia 65
Malamed, Connie 24, 28, 84
Mallan, Kerry 107
Manara, Milo 120, *121*
Mareis, Claudia 13, 73
Marx, Karl 91
Masuda, Takahiko 124
Mau, Bruce 91
Maviyane-Davies, Chaz xi, 118
Maximalism 99
McCloud, Scott xiii, 12, 23-29, 52, 85, 119-122
Mecha Fetus Visual Blog. 102
Medley, Stuart 24, 30, *46*, *48*, 60, 61, *93*
Meggs, Phil 3, 27, 57, 81
metapicture *see* picture
Miall Smith, Jenny 84
Mies van der Rohe, Ludwig 56
Miller, J. Abbott 2, 17-20, 42, 59, 61, 90, 92, 108
Mitchell, W.J.T. 4, 5, 26, 120, 127
Mirzoeff, Nicholas 10
Modley, Rudolf 24, 82
Modernism 17, 58, 62, 64, 73
de Moor, Bob 119
Mori, Matsuhiro 113
Morris, Charles 18, 82
Moustafa, Ahmed 112
Müller, Lars 61, 62, 75
Müller and Hess *77*

Müller-Brockmann, Josef 29, 58-59, 61-62, 75, 77
Müller-Lyer Illusion 44, *45*

N

Nagel, Patrick *72*
Nakata, Robert 67
Neue Schweizer Grafik 2, 56, 58, 61, 62, 67, 75, 77, 84, 96
Neurath, Otto 73, 81-84
Nippon Design Centre 73
noise (in visual communication) 1, 28, 33, 43-44, 74, 84, 89, 105
norms (*see also* caricature) 47, 51, 114, 126, 128
NORM (typographers) 73, 123-126

O

object constancy 18, 30, 47, 52-53, 130
object hypothesis 36, 39, 40, 42, 51
Olympics
    Munich 73, 82, 87
    Tokyo 73
ornament 102-103

P

Patton, Judy 3, 115
perception 6, 14-19, 28, 30, 34-43, 53, 81-84, 92, 130
perceptual constancies 6, 38-47, 109, 119
pharmaceutical industry 59-61
Phunk Studio 68
pictogram. xvi, 8, 29, 79-83, 87, 123, 130

picture
    definition of 4-9
    metapicture 120, 123
    verb equivalence 90, 92, 97
photography
    de-identified subjects 110-111
    definition 7, 9, 10
    documentary photography 7-11, 59, 89, 109
    specificity 18, 57, 89, 109, 110
    stock photography 18, 90

Photoshop software 72
Plato 51, 56, 112
Popper, Karl 39
Poracsky, Joseph 3, 115
post-modernism 61-65, 95, 103, 126-127
Poynor, Rick 62-67, 70, 104
Psychophysics 47
Purvis, Alston 3, 27, 57, 81
Purvis, Tom *71*

R

Ramachandran, Vilayanur 51-52, 101
Rand, Paul 61, 64-65
Rathgeb. Marcus 52, 82-83
Rauschenberger, Robert 41
recognition continuum 53
realism
    concrete to abstract 24-25, 130
    less-real-than-real 28, 34, 36, 37
    realism continuum 23-31, 36, 53, 79, 84, 85, 123, 124, 129-132
    specific to universal 26-29

Reinhard, Erik. 49, 53
Resnick, Elizabeth xi, 118
Rhodes, Gillian 30, 47-48
Rinzen 14, 68, 70, 97-107
Robertson, Paul 102

Rodchenko 56
Rodman, Lilita 26
Roska, Botond 45
Rosling, Hans 92
Rowland, Anna 56
Ruddigkeit, Raban 96

S

Samara, Timothy 65
Sanders Illusion 44, *45*
de Sausmarez, Maurice 12, 15, 125
schema 6, 8, 12, 39-41, 81, 98, 112, 130
Scheuermann, Arne xi, 19, 132
Schonell, Fred 92
screen-printing 70
semiotics 18, 20
sensation 12, 17, 30, 38, 44
senses 51-52, 85
Shannon, Claude Elwood 28, 33
shape constancy 39
Shaughnessy, Adrian 14
Shaw, Bernard 59
Shell logo 75
silhouette 30, 36-40, 53, 81-82
  airline safety cards 117
  Iraq poster 118
size constancy 39
Skolos, Nancy 60, 64
Skopec, David xi
social theory 91-93
Sontag, Susan 10-11, 20, 33, 85, 91
Spiekermann, Erik 4, 125
Stermer, Dougald 13
stereopsis 34
Stoichita, Victor 37
Swiss Design Network xi, 132
Swiss Typography School *see* Neue Schweizer Grafik
symbol 24-30, 75, 82-86

synaesthesia 12, 51, 101, 126, 128
system of seeing 86-87

T

Thomas, Patrick 97-98, 105-106
Tintin 119-120, 41
Tschichold, Jan 58
Tufte, Edward 74-75, 79, 81, 85
Twemlow, Alice 102
typography
  Elements of typographic style 5
  picture and type on the continuum 24-27, 123-125
  rules 5, 66, 123
  word shape 125-126

U

unreal 30, 112
Ulm School 19, 58, 83
Uncanny Valley 113

V

Van Leeuwen, Theo 19, 132
Viennese Method 73
visual literacy (*see also* graphicacy) 3, 19, 60, 95-97, 107-109
  no exact equivalence between verbal and visual communication
  Visual Literacy White Paper 107
visual system 11, 14, 30, 33-48, 53, 81, 83, 96, 108, 125, 129-130
visuality 91, 95, 103, 112, 115, 123, 131

W

Warde, Beatrice xv
Weaver, Warren 28, 33
Wedell, Thomas 60, 64
Werblin, Frank 45
Wertheimer, M 42
Wileman, Ralph. 23-27, 85, 90, 107-108
Wilson, Michael 27
Wlassikoff, Michel 57
Woodiwiss, Anthony 91
Wurman, Richard S 3, 67, 74-78, 92

Y

Yamashita, Yoshiro 73, 82
Yantis, Steven 41
Yokoyama, Akira *114*
Young, Emily 3, 115
Yuki, Masaki 124

Z

Zwimpfer, M *39*

CPSIA information can be obtained
at www.ICGtesting.com
Printed in the USA
LVHW081542171219
640805LV00004B/302/P